CRITICISM IN ACTION
A critical symposium on Modern Poems

Edited by
MAURICE HUSSEY

LONGMANS

LONGMANS, GREEN AND CO LTD
London and Harlow

Associated companies, branches and representatives throughout the world

This edition © Longmans, Green and Co Ltd 1969
First published 1969

SBN 582 34170 1

ACKNOWLEDGEMENTS

The publishers are grateful to the following for permission to reproduce copyright material:

The Trustees of the Thomas Hardy Estate and Macmillan and Co Ltd for *Overlooking the River Stour* and *Sheep Boy* from *The Collected Poems of Thomas Hardy*.

Laurence Pollinger Ltd for *Snake* and *Last Lesson of the Afternoon* by D. H. Lawrence.

Rupert Hart-Davis Ltd for *The Old Age of Michelangelo* by Frank Prince.

The author and A. P. Watt Ltd for *End of Play* and *Counting the Beats* by Robert Graves.

MacGibbon and Kee Ltd for *First Hymn to Lenin* and *By Wauchopeside* by Hugh MacDiarmid.

Chatto and Windus Ltd for *The Violet* and Stand Vol. 8 No. 1, 1966 for *Worm* by Jon Silkin; author's agents and Chatto and Windus Ltd. for *Chagrin* and *Returning We Hear the Larks* by Isaac Rosenberg from his *Collected Poems*.

Faber and Faber Ltd for *An Otter* and *Hawk Roosting* by Ted Hughes from *Lupercal*; for *Waking Early Sunday Morning* by Robert Lowell from *Near The Ocean*; and for *Beasts* and *All Souls* by Richard Wilbur.

Donald Davie and Fantasy Press for *Remembering The Thirties* © 1955 Donald Davie reprinted from *New and Selected Poems* by permission of Wesleyan University Press.

Routledge & Kegan Paul Ltd for *Hornet* and *Low Lands* by Donald Davie.

Wedding Wind and *Church Going* by Philip Larkin are reprinted from *The Less Deceived* by permission of the Marvell Press.

Printed in Great Britain by
Spottiswoode, Ballantyne and Co Ltd
London and Colchester

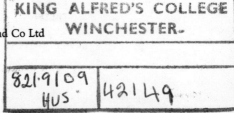

CONTENTS

INTRODUCTION

I

CRITICISM IN ACTION is not a cross-section of the history of twentieth-century poetry. It is a symposium intended to provide a series of critical performances on modern examples. None of the works selected is avant-garde or taken from that increasing body of poems written especially for public performance, but they include Robert Lowell's *Waking Early Sunday Morning*—highly contemporary in theme and sensibility and, as Mr Lucie-Smith shows, a dramatic monologue of great distinction.

Of the three most distinguished poets writing in English in the earlier years of the century, two have been much appraised and one largely neglected. T. S. Eliot and W. B. Yeats have each been made the subject of scholarly industry, while the latter is already the subject also of a regular festival at Sligo where progress reports are read. Thomas Hardy, the only indisputable English writer of the three, has been far more discussed as a Victorian novelist than as a modern poet, as is essentially the case with D. H. Lawrence. Hardy's great output of verse has won the acclaim of a number of living poets such as Graves, W. H. Auden and Philip Larkin, the last (see p. 59) having defended every page in the large *Collected Poems* volume for showing technical achievement and command of a wide variety of experience. Eliot and Yeats we agreed not to include in the present book, preferring to stress the versatility of Hardy by picking three unfamiliar poems.

Coming nearer the halfway mark of our century we have little difficulty in finding published commentary in book form on Dylan Thomas and W. H. Auden. Once more it was decided not to use any of their poems here. Empson was excluded with more regret but because his virtuoso poems encourage a virtuoso analytical technique in which the novice could only partake as an onlooker.

When the average length of a critique is taken into account, it will be seen that the selection of living poets, considered as being at the height of their powers, had to be a small one. The work of such poets as Thom Gunn, Charles Tomlinson and Peter Porter, for instance, was excluded for this reason alone.

It is to be hoped that the depth of the analyses will more than compensate for the omission of certain poets. As has been said at the outset, this is primarily a series of critical performances in which the writers have for once been given the space to suggest what engages them most deeply in poetry of their own choice and why the reader might agree with their judgments.

All that we do as readers must stem from our approach to new poems one at a time. We may go on to do three things: to notice the characteristics and self-consistencies of a writer over a wide range; to venture more widely into the period to look for the shared characteristics that make up the literary context; to place a poem within the development of its genre or tradition. All these we do with increasing skill and range as critical readers, but all the time we start from the personal critical response to the individual poem and the analytical strategy that we have learned to wield.

Critics may lend a hand in these explorations but they are middlemen who have to commit themselves upon complex poems and then retire leaving the individual to form his own judgment. Not imagining that they are replacing the creative writers, they know that, provided their interpretations are used carefully, they can offer a number of tips to less well qualified students.

So fast is the development of modern literary experience that students who can take nothing from one poet at the beginning of a year may find that his statements are both powerful and inevitable in expression by the end of it. Since the end of an academic year often brings with it an examination when we are asked to sit and deliver our opinions on unsigned passages of verse and prose, it is a realistic way to end this symposium and give it shape to invite an examiner, Professor Welland, to draw our conclusion for us. I think it will be seen from his chapter that there is nothing dogmatic in his approach to literary examination. He is anxious to reward the candidate who can express his opinions clearly and cogently, no matter what disagreements the examiner and the candidate might have over details of interpretation.

Delivering one's opinion under examination pressure can be one more proof that good critical analysis is a personal matter. The bad critic forgets that the poet's technical abilities are at the service of his power to communicate. Indeed, the imperfect examination candidate approaches the status of a computer. A machine can be programmed to notice such externals as length and variety of sentence structure, even to write a Latin hexameter or neo-Joycean English, but it cannot use a more delicate system of values. The weaker candidate may conduct similarly a census upon the rhymes and metres of the poem, jump for joy at the alliterations and imagine a high concentration of onomatopoeia, but cannot convincingly relate these to the embodying and enactive processes whereby precise details are taken into the poetry and assist in the communication. The good critic at all times will be much more responsive. He will consider what the prescribed poem is about and then feeling 'along the line' report on the integrity of the writer's engagement with his theme by means of deft quotation.

The analyses that follow are intended to serve as models to help the reader to leave behind the mechanical stage ('classifying and analysing of books in an imitation-botanical fashion' as D. H. Lawrence called it) in order to become a more perfect critic. This is the aim of the writers in the pages ahead. This is the way the book should be read.

II

English literary criticism stretches back to the Renaissance yet few of its early representatives make interesting reading except to the specialist. Their writings are replete with classical authorities but often short of practical demonstrations of criticism in action. The first great exception and major critic is Samuel Johnson, who possessed and revealed strong standards of judgment and wrote a critical rhetoric whose authoritarianism suited his Augustan readers. His *Preface to Shakespeare* is the most memorable piece of Shakespeare criticism yet written, while in his *Life of Pope* he presented an extended study of Pope's epitaphs in which the detailed precise criticism of our own day is prefigured.

Johnson wrote at a time when education was derived from the authority of the classics and we view him from one in which education is free and the arts a major preoccupation of the universities. Before 1914, however, English was barely a university subject at all. The Edwardian, imperialist and Georgian styles of poetry neither needed nor survived close analysis; appreciation then was indistinguishable from gossip. In those years *The Times Literary Supplement* and other journals encouraged such thin Romanticism that C. K. Stead has written: 'no new poetry of substance could be written by men who remained dependent on the approval of popular reviewers and the general public of this time' (*The New Poetic*). As so often happens, changes were hastened by the war, taking the form we now know as The Modern Movement in the Arts associated with the names of Eliot, Pound, Joyce, Schoenberg, Stravinsky and Cocteau. In the field of English poetry there were, among others, the Imagists (Anglo-American in personnel) whose work emphasised poetic images and drew on the flexibility of free verse, but lacked formal qualities recognised and accepted by the majority of potential readers. Like the early Romantics, they felt the need to re-educate their public, create and foster the taste by which they could be judged.

If we consider for a moment the ideas of literary history put forward by Ezra Pound we see that universities could not long stand apart from such developments in the arts, though they might not go all the way to meet them. Pound issued a challenge that not even the new universities of the 1960s have taken up. He rejected the work of Spenser, Milton, Dryden, Blake and the whole of the last century, while demanding the adoption into a curriculum of Provençal poetry and the classical literature of China. It is difficult to see a central and all-connecting core in his proposals, and his friend, T. S. Eliot, had much more deserved success.

Eliot passed from the stage of being castigated as a 'literary bolshevik' to that of the leading intellectual in England remarkably swiftly. Though he was not associated with any university in particular, his influence as both poet and critic was immense during his lifetime. His poetry demanded and received close analytical reading, his essays provided many acceptable propositions

4

which had the effect of reshaping both verse and criticism for decades.

Powerful assistance for the writers of the 1920s came from the posthumous publication of the poetry of Gerard Manley Hopkins and the rehabilitation of the poetry of Donne and the Metaphysicals. Those reading widely for the first time then must have experienced, in an imprecise manner, the resemblances between living and dead poets, a mingling of metaphysical and modern, as a challenge to previously held ideas of literary history. They all seemed equally new and the ahistorical critical studies that were developed at the universities probably served to emphasise their similarity. The movement towards practical criticism, described above, insists upon local and analysable qualities in poems rather than such principles as the gradual development of style. Not, of course, that these can be neglected, but the essential newness of every poem for the reader is a feature of the technique which has, in America, been termed 'new criticism'.

Eliot's insistence on the primary importance of poetic traditions, and Leavis's later more detailed investigations of how these may be identified, guaranteed that a historical sense was not lacking. What was to be dismissed was the imitation-botanical, artificial-historical academic ways of cataloguing. A challenge to personal involvement took its place in the study of English and was responsible for its prolonged success. Not since the slow abandonment of classical rhetoric as the authority in schools and universities has there been so fruitful a literary training introduced: different though it is, critical analysis may be regarded as our modern form of education in rhetoric.

I. A. Richards, originally a student of psychology and philosophy, is with some reason considered the originator of critical studies within the English Faculty of Cambridge University. He turned away from such other representative men of his day as Bertrand Russell, G. E. Moore and Ludwig Wittgenstein, none of whom was particularly interested in literature, and developed the literary techniques explained in his books *Principles of Literary Criticism* (1924) and *Practical Criticism* (1929). From about 1919 he issued sheets of unsigned poems to undergraduates soliciting and codifying their unsigned comments. It was his main interest to see what emotional and other built-in resistances to types of poetry were at work to prevent highly educated and articulate young people of the period from developing their literary taste. The psychological element in this undertaking is still more apparent in his later work, but if he had something of the consumer-researcher about him he was the first to schematise the methods of modern literary education. He used contemporary literature alongside that of the past and has been acknowledged as one of the formative figures in the university study of English Literature. As seen today his work is the beginning of a significant movement. The technique depended on working in small groups with a tutor. Personal tastes and therefore ultimately the personal, private life were being cultivated; social ends, apart from carrying on the same education afterwards, were of less importance. This work contains an opposition to authoritarianism that still needs to be written into a future revision of English educational priorities in 1969.

When Richards left England about 1930 it fell to F. R. Leavis to extend the range of literary criticism at Cambridge so that its influence was felt far outside it. The achievements of this important teacher cannot be summed up here except to say that in all his work the process of criticism (he ignores the adjective 'practical'), close discussion is central. Precise demonstration is invoked by him when all literary judgments are to be made, favourable or unfavourable, preferring the good to the bad or the better to the merely good. Matthew Arnold wrote that 'first-rate criticism has a permanent value greater than that of any but the first-rate works of poetry and art'. One can only state that, more than any other, Professor Leavis has fulfilled the Arnoldian requirements by the integrity of his critical work, whether in the twenty volumes of *Scrutiny* which he edited, or in other independent writings. In his hands the critical performance became a perfectly controlled teaching and research method, one that was intended to replace too great a concentration upon *facts about* literature and to offer the improvement of the expression of a reader's careful response to literary art as the reason for the undertaking.

Space prohibits any attempt to assess the work of younger critics beyond acknowledging the existence of a large corpus of criticism published in the United States. Colleges such as Vanderbilt and

Kenyon, and writers such as Lionel Trilling, Cleanth Brooks and Robert Penn Warren merit close attention from historians of criticism. Nothing can be said here about the parallel development of American poetry, though it is represented in this collection by the work of three writers. The introduction of critical analysis into school courses, first for the purpose of university entrance examinations and then, as is the equivocal experience in England, for Advanced Level papers, will be much more familiar to present readers. They may equally regret the notion that has grown up that what is not demanded in an examination will not be taught, but be consoled by the fact that candidates reach distinction as readily in this as in any other part of the paper more subject to memory than to scrupulousness of response and swift cogency of statement.

Another speculation for the historian of criticism will be upon the effects of training yearly hundreds and thousands of students to recognise false notes in verbal communication. It may ultimately affect poetic style, or may already have done so. This also is a point we cannot pursue.

What is of more moment is the recent reaction against seminars in criticism in English universities. Oxford, which recognises no literature more modern than 1900, has never favoured it, but in some of the new universities, with the adoption of wider arts degrees than the single-subject type (and the introduction of sociology, psychology and other modern studies), there is a reaction away from the more intensely time-consuming work of criticism and learning how to assign dates to unsigned passages of writing from internal evidence. It is too early to assess this move, but the following list of universities, while not exhaustive, gives a guide to those in which undergraduate work in English concentrates most fully upon practical criticism. Other English faculties may encourage what Leavis has called 'a discipline of thought that is at the same time a discipline in scrupulous sensitiveness of response to delicate organizations of feeling, sensation and imagery', but the published syllabuses provide us with one dozen:

Bangor	Durham	Liverpool	Sheffield
Bristol	Hull	Newcastle	Sussex
Cambridge	Leicester	Nottingham	Swansea

III

It is unnecessary to introduce individually the chapters that follow. The first two—by Dr Rodway and Mr Hobsbaum—both offer definitions of the process of criticism to which we direct readers. Every one will profit from these two restatements for young critics, even though he is likely to have made an approach to criticism already, possibly through one of the excellent books of practical criticism for school use such as *Reading and Discrimination* by Denys Thompson or the more recent *Reading and Response* by R. P. Hewitt; or since it has been emphasised that the process is inevitably a person-to-person one, through sheets of passages drawn up by a teacher with his own slant upon the problems of literary analysis. The chapters from Hardy to Lowell may be read in any order depending whether date, length or subject-matter is the dominant factor.

Each contributor may be relied on to have picked out what interests him most in the work under scrutiny, and not only a single thread in it: his hope will be to secure our agreement to his views. Thus, while Sydney Bolt has pinpointed the claims of rhythm and movement in Robert Graves's work he also has space to suggest the consistency of this writer over his long career and the place of his output within the traditions of amatory poetry in English. The reader can follow the same emphasis on poetic movement, for instance, in the chapters on Edward Thomas and Philip Larkin. Imagery is probably the most immediately attractive element in poetry, the most sensitive index to the poet's imagination, but it is rhythm that is most commonly discussed by the young critic with the least conviction. These points should be noted with greater care and less uninformed subjectivity.

The Editor is especially pleased to be in a position to offer what would seem to be the only substantial analysis in print of one of the long dramatic monologues of Frank Prince. Michael Black's account on pp. 144–162, has the poet's own support. To my personal view, intentionally provocative, *The Old Age of Michelangelo* is the best long poem published in England since T. S. Eliot's *Four Quartets*. All the participating critics deserve grateful thanks, not only for their essays but in some cases for bearing with the rest of us in patience. They are united, coming as they do from every sector of the field of education, in believing in practical criticism as the basis of the study of the verbal arts, one through which the student refines his aesthetic pleasure and immeasurably strengthens his judgment.

MAURICE HUSSEY

RICHARD WILBUR
Beasts
In the Elegy Season

Commentary by Allan Rodway

Beasts

Beasts in their major freedom
Slumber in peace tonight. The gull on his ledge
Dreams in the guts of himself the moon-plucked waves below,
And the sunfish leans on a stone, slept
5   By the lyric water,

In which the spotless feet
Of deer make dulcet splashes, and to which
The ripped mouse, safe in the owl's talon, cries
Concordance. Here there is no such harm
10   And no such darkness

As the selfsame moon observes
Where, warped in window-glass, it sponsors now
The werewolf's painful change. Turning his head away
On the sweaty bolster, he tries to remember
15   The mood of manhood,

But lies at last, as always,
Letting it happen, the fierce fur soft to his face,
Hearing with sharper ears the wind's exciting minors,
The leaves' panic, and the degradation
20   Of the heavy streams.

Meantime, at high windows
Far from thicket and pad-fall, suitors of excellence
Sigh and turn from their work to construe again the painful
Beauty of heaven, the lucid moon
25   And the risen hunter,

Making such dreams for men
As told will break their hearts as always, bringing
Monsters into the city, crows on the public statues,
Navies fed to the fish in the dark
30   Unbridled waters.

In the Elegy Season

Haze, char, and the weather of All Souls':
A giant absence mopes upon the trees:
Leaves cast in casual potpourris
Whisper their scents from pits and cellar-holes.

5   Or brewed in gulleys, steeped in wells, they spend
In chilly steam their last aromas, yield
From shallow hells a revenance of field
And orchard air. And now the envious mind

Which could not hold the summer in my head
10   While bounded by that blazing circumstance
Parades these barrens in a golden trance,
Remembering the wealthy season dead,

And by an autumn inspiration makes
A summer all its own. Green boughs arise
15   Through all the boundless backward of the eyes,
And the soul bathes in warm conceptual lakes.

Less proud than this, my body leans an ear
Past cold and colder weather after wings'
Soft commotion, the sudden race of springs,
20   The goddess' tread heard on the dayward stair,

Longs for the brush of the freighted air, for smells
Of grass and cordial lilac, for the sight
Of green leaves building into the light
And azure water hoisting out of wells.

Beneath the procedural problems that beset literary critics lie two major problems of theory. The first is to do with the literature's mode of existence, the second with the critic's mode of apprehension.

Works of literature—unlike painting, sculpture, and even music—have no significant material existence at all: their significance is 'all in the mind'. True apprehension of that significance, in the work as a whole, clearly depends on a correct interpretation of its parts—but since these are non-material parts their nature is unfixed, and it is often impossible to decide what sort of parts they are without comprehending the wholes of which they form parts.

So literary criticism is a vain attempt to do the impossible with the non-existent? Not quite; but it does have to steer a difficult way between the Charybdis of arrogant opinion and the Scylla of slavish submission to authority. Critical methods, then, should allow for these problems of theory and the practical dangers associated with them.

If a work's significance is all in the mind, how are we to see that what does take place in the mind when it is read is what should, that it is a product neither of arrogance nor of slavishness but of a controlled responsiveness? Well, first by cultivating knowledge of our own times, prejudices and predispositions of temperament, and knowledge of other people and other periods; secondly, by 'practical criticism': the criticism of works whose authorship is unrevealed, or works of a poet like Wilbur as yet unburdened by an established reputation—criticism, that is to say, which is forced to be independent. It could still, of course, turn out to be unsupported opinionation rather than *justifiable* assessment. To start with technical interpretation or description, rather than evaluation, is the best way of avoiding that. So self-knowledge, situation-knowledge, and (the thing that is relevant here) a technical method deal with the first problem. But what of the problem of parts and whole?

In the case of a careful writer like Wilbur, clearly in control of his material, 'coherence' carries most weight as evidence of valid interpretation. In such cases the interpretation that has to strain probability in order to account for various features of the poem is unlikely to be right. However, it is not an infallible test even for carefully written short poems. Take parody, for instance. A good parody of, say, a poem by Wordsworth would be as coherent as the original. Proper appreciation, though, would depend on the reader's knowing what *sort* of coherent whole this was (namely, parodic). Only with that knowledge could the reader correctly interpret the quality of various parts as being praiseworthy comic caricature rather than the deplorable coarse exaggeration they appeared to be. And it might well be that he could not reasonably be expected to recognise the whole as parody—let alone appreciate its merits as such—without external knowledge (namely, of the Wordsworth poem). Sometimes, too, it could happen that *only* peripheral, 'scholarly' knowledge would lead to that interdependent apprehension of parts-and-whole required for valid assessment. Take this poem:

> She dwelt among the untrodden ways
>   Beside the springs of Dove,
> A maid whom there were none to praise
>   And very few to love:
>
> A violet by a mossy stone
>   Half hidden from the eye,
> Fair as a star, when only one
>   Is shining in the sky.
>
> She lived unknown, and few could know
>   When Lucy ceased to be;
> But she is in her grave, and oh
>   The difference to me!

Now this can be read in two different ways, so as to give two coherent but contradictory significances. Is it as a whole mocking or elegiac? On the first assumption we read the parts ironically—especially the last line and a half of each stanza (or, to put it the other way round, if we take these parts to be ironical the whole becomes a lampoon on Lucy). On the second assumption we read them movingly. Nothing in the language compels us to one reading rather than the other. What items of circumstantial evidence there are more or less cancel out. Yet, of course, everyone knows that the right reading—that which would have been adopted by an intelligent contemporary reader of Wordsworth—is the serious one. But how do we 'know'? Surely only by knowing, perhaps subconsciously, that Wordsworth did not have a macabre sense of humour, or indeed any sense of humour; by knowing the characteristic tone of the other Lucy poems; by knowing that the ironic was never a Wordsworthian mood. This would not be a poem suitable for the pedagogical exercise of practical criticism.

For poems that demand little or no external knowledge, and are presented in a practical criticism situation where it is not available (to give a lead, or to mislead), there is only one way to resolve the chameleonlike relationship of parts and whole. It is the hard way of working bit by bit in a constant alternation of experiment and hypothesis, with frequent triangulation, by form, tone or theme—for literary wholes are complex—as a safeguard against going astray, and then insensibly straining the later evidence instead of altering the hypothesis. The evidence of each line as it comes tends to validate or invalidate that tentative hypothesis about the sort of whole to which the title and previous lines have given rise (especially in so far as the evidence from one aspect, say the thematic, is supported or not by evidence from the tonal or formal aspects). This procedure may and ought to be adopted, of course, even if we are not doing practical criticism, as a sort of general triangulation to check whatever appraisal seems to be supported by the external information.

That all this leads only to the most valid *interpretation* that the nature of literature permits does not matter as much as it might seem to. If we have revealed what seems to be genuinely the public poem, not a private misreading, and have brought to light features that might have escaped notice, we have done all that is *literarily* required: made a small new world available.

All critical evidence is necessarily circumstantial. Whether we accumulate it in the way described, in order to escape the basic dilemmas, or more aesthetically in order to refine our perception of certain qualities, the two procedural problems that face us are these: where to start and when to stop. Here only good sense and sensibility can help. As everything is ultimately fused with everything else in a poem, a start at any point will lead eventually to every other; it is simply that some starting places will be more convenient than others. As for when to stop—well, before dissection becomes murder; but there are no rules for deciding when that is. Happily, even poems that seem to have been murdered often come to life again, if they are laid aside till the overzealous analysis has settled at the bottom of the mind, and are then reread for pleasure—but, presumably, with heightened awareness.

Beasts. Briefly, what sort of whole is this poem—mimetic? Does it

16

try to make an imaginatively solid world, that of beasts? The first stanza might tempt us to think so, but hardly the last. Anyway, what about the 'major' freedom of the first line? Major as compared with what? And what about the general structure? The first two stanzas are the only ones that deal exclusively with beasts; the next two are about a man-beast; the last two largely about man. Is it then a didactic poem? Does it purport to *say* something rather than *be* something? Has it a theme? To put it bluntly, does such a title for a poem clearly not only about beasts mean we are being told that men are beasts, and bad beasts at that? Certainly the movement is downward, from 'lyric' to 'unbridled' water, peaceful to night-marish dreams, and the word 'degradation' for the descending streams seems too striking not to be significant. Suppose we were to say: this is indeed a didactic poem, whose moral theme is that the nature of beasts is harmonious while man's is discordant. This certainly gets support from 'moon-plucked', 'lyric', 'dulcet', and 'concordance' in the first two stanzas, and 'painful' in the third and fifth; moreover the musical implications of 'major' and 'minors' hint a change of key, a darkening of tone. But what of the 'ripped' mouse? And why does the moon feature, differently, in each section? Simply as a unifying agent? Or is it a symbolic property, acting as a kind of visual pun on *lunar* and *lunatic*? Surely, this is likely, for if this poem is didactic it is not so in either a narrative or an argumentative way; it tries to combine the intellectual benefits of didacticism with the material benefits of mimesis—and only symbolism combines the concrete and the abstract. Let us then rephrase the theme as follows: 'The harmonious, if ruthless, nature of beasts contrasts favourably with the doubly discordant nature of man, warped by physical and spiritual lunacy.'

The moon, of course, is *also* a unifying agent, helping to ensure that the three thematic (and tonal) sections are parts of a well-integrated whole, contributing to that sense of unity-in-variety which is so important a part of aesthetic effect. Another such factor is that of sleep. This, too, is a repeated but varying motif. The sleep of beasts is peaceful; their 'major freedom' is freedom from pain, degradation and terror. We are told, as a thematic assertion that they 'slumber in peace'. Tonally, this statement is reinforced by the musical words mentioned and by the pun on 'spotless' (free of sin as well as clean). And formally, it is both implied and accounted for by the kind of grammar used. Wilbur should have said the gull 'Dreams . . . *of* the moon-plucked waves below' because dreams, having no physical dimension, cannot accommodate real objects. He says the sunfish '(is) slept By the lyric water'. But 'to sleep' is an intransitive verb and cannot have a passive mood, since something you only do yourself cannot be done to you. He should have written 'sleeps', at any rate if he wanted to be grammatical. Clearly he did not want to be, but rather wanted the odd grammatical form to impress on us the unsayable difference of the beasts—so much a part of nature that the fish is not separable from the water, the dream from the guts, nor the guts from the waves that feed them. That is why the ripped mouse paradoxically 'cries Concordance', and is 'safe' in the owl's talon in two senses: held firm, and fulfilling its destined (but happily unanticipated) role in the natural order.

In the fourth stanza 'degradation' (line 19) is the obvious pun. A formal device, choosing to fuse two meanings rather than separate them; a tonal device (since, taken in context, together with 'heavy', it suggests the *blood*stream), and a contribution to the thematic development. In so far as it is connected with water, it is part of another motif (again a changing one, and therefore part of form*). A less obvious pun is that on 'panic' (to do with the lustful earth-god, Pan). The warping window-glass suggests those round bottle-glass windows associated with legendary castles or sinister old mansions; it symbolises man's distortion of nature, accounts for the disturbed rest, and prepares for 'degradation'. The paradox of '*fierce* fur *soft* to his face' and the transferred epithet (from wolf to fur) both formally mimic the larger statement of change in this section as a whole. Somewhere in the background there seems to be a suppressed image of masturbation—suppressed, one might guess, because the author merely wished to refine on the complex mood that would accompany *anything* in human experience that the werewolf might symbolise.

In the fifth stanza the moon is 'lucid', seen through 'high', not warping windows; but it is associated with 'the risen hunter',

* *How* things are said as opposed to *what* is said—though, as we see, these are often distinguishable only for critical convenience.

18

Sagittarius: like Pan half beast and half man—and an archer, so not a natural hunter like the owl. Similarly, the dreams of the last stanza are not natural like those of the beasts. They are *made* by the 'suitors of excellence'; who are not in harmony with the heavens but trying to 'construe' the 'painful' beauty of the moon and stars. Presumably these are the idealists—poets, philosophers, theologians, political theorists—who move too far to the spiritual end of the human spectrum, as the werewolf-type moves too far to the animal end, with equally 'lunatic' results. The grammatical parallel, 'making . . ., bringing . . .', suggests that the disasters mentioned are not part of the 'dreams' (prophetic threats, so to speak) but actual results of idealistic speculation—the disasters of religious or ideological or romantic-nationalist wars.

Only the stanza form is repeated *without* thematic variation; all other unifying motifs take some colouring from the different parts. They can afford to, for the stanza form is strongly unifying, the development is unforced, and much of the supporting detail wonderfully delicate. Note, as a concluding example, that the last word of the last stanza could perfectly well have matched the last word of the first stanza exactly. That it does not is not merely elegant variation. 'Waters' is more disunified than 'water' (as 'lyric' suggests a single harmony and 'unbridled' a stormy herd of white horses). Down to the very last words Wilbur controls and combines sense and form; thus having the poem itself act as an example of the integration that its total significance indicates to be desirable.

In the Elegy Season. An elegy. So perhaps we should start with the tonal aspect of this poem. But what is its tone? If the first two stanzas are 'elegy' enough, are not the next two 'Elgar'—imbued with pomp and circumstance—and the last two positively cele-bratory? Have we indeed jumped to a wrong conclusion in supposing it an elegy at all? That noun acts as an adjective in the title. Is this a piece of wit (in one of the older senses: intellectual play)? Is it teasing us by holding out the idea of an elegy, only to snatch it back with the suggestion that the word merely describes a kind of season? And what kind? One that is itself sad (elegiac), or one suitable for writing elegies on the past year? In fact, it turns out, Wilbur gives us the elegiac *tone* of autumn in the first section (of what turns out to be again a work in three parts of two stanzas each), goes on to an elegy for summer, with a very unelegiac tone, and then switches to a tone of celebration for what has not yet happened! Clearly the title's teasing ambiguity was not accidental. Nevertheless, we can profitably pursue the matter of tone further—noting, however, that the tonal blocks correspond with thematic blocks introduced by logical links: 'And now', 'Less proud than this', and these in turn with formal qualities appropriate to the envious 'mind' and less proud 'body'. But in the first section the tonal aspect is dominant. In formal quality it is neither predominantly physical nor mental; nor does it so clearly make a conceptual point as the other two sections. In them the thematic, formal and tonal are equal partners.

Bearing in mind, then, a rather negative idea of the whole—not simply elegiac or celebratory, not obviously either the more mimetic or didactic—let us examine the first part. 'Haze, char, and the weather of All Souls':' clearly sets up an autumnal feeling, a sense of the tonal quality of the day. But once again it is impossible to separate tone and form and referential meaning (which can come under the other umbrella-term, theme). The fact that the first two words and the last two are both stressed and long-vowelled slows down the line, so that, in combination with the implications of 'Haze', and 'char' (presumably charred wood), there is a sense of looking round, taking in the scene. 'All Souls'' gives just a hint of ghostliness in the air—the hazy weather being apt enough in more than one sense. That hint, of course, is brilliantly and wittily picked up—after the phantasmal 'chilly steam' has been added to 'Haze' and 'brewed' and 'steeped' have brought in faint aromas of witch's potions—by the word 'revenance'. As striking and unexpected as 'degradation' in *Beasts*, it insists on its literal meaning (cp. *revenir*), a 'coming back', and carries along with that the idea of a revenant or apparition from the 'shallow hells'. All these words, then, add tonal touches to an impressionist picture.

However, they are not only elegiac but also, paradoxically, witty; the tonal colour of this section, ambiguous as the title, changes like shot silk according to the way you look at it. The tone, in fact, expresses the paradoxical quality of autumn, the ghostliness of presences that are made of absences—beautifully hit off in the second line's metaphor of the striking absence of leaves as a giant, invisible,

20

forlorn bird. The same subtlety of wit is evident in the synesthesia of 'Whisper their scents' (where the sound is a sonic reference to the rustling leaves while the sense speaks of their more ghostly emanation, as scent). And, of course, 'potpourris' (mixtures of dead leaves, flower petals and herbs kept in bowls, in past times) is perfect both visually and nostalgically. Negative emotion and ghostly being, spiced by a wit aware of the dangers of delicious nostalgia, are what this section evokes. Since the other sections are less dominantly tonal it might be as well to approach them via matters of general structure.

Clearly there is a temporal movement from present (late autumn) to past (summer) to future (through winter to spring). These sections are concerned, respectively, with emotional, mental and bodily reactions to the season; the narrative, moving from impersonal and intangible to personal and tangible, is enabled by the logical links mentioned to retain the immediacy that comes from using the present tense, despite the time shifts. In the first section the most ethereal of the senses, smell, predominates, in the second, sight (and paradoxically, sight of much more tangible things than in the first, although it is only in memory), in the third, probably touch (the closest of the senses). But one has to say 'probably' because smell, sight and sound are also insisted on. In fact, this poem does not so much develop as *accumulate*. Its stages are less of argument than of mounting vitality. If *Beasts* was, finally, didactic in kind despite some appearance of mimesis, *In the Elegy Season* is finally mimetic in kind despite some appearance of a didactic theme (to do with the human tendency to live more vitally in memory and anticipation than in present reality). There is not only a progressive increase in tangibility, but also a progressive increase in *movement* (and a consequent sense of vitality), and then in the last stanza 'smells' in the first line, 'sight' in the second, 'building' (a muscular image) in the third recapitulate in order the predominant sense impressions of the three sections.

It is as well to recall, however, that poems may well have items of local texture that are aesthetically pleasing, though they may not be *essential* to the theme. Indeed a poem without any textural superfluity, any aesthetic sense of delight in language almost for its own sake might appear too starkly functional. In this poem, the clearest example is the word 'conceptual'. It is, of course, *appropriate* to the theme. But 'imaginary' would have been equally so, indeed rather more so—in fact so obviously so that one gets a sense of verbal pleasure from Wilbur's avoiding it. Similarly, the latent image of the summer as a wealthy relative, and the 'envious mind' as a young heir glorying in his inheritance rather than mourning the dead gives a witty twist to the second 'elegiac' section, and supports it formally by a parading rhythm emphasised by the 'b' alliteration, and tonally by the overtones of 'Parades' and (in this context) the absurdly romantic 'inspiration'.

In the third section we might note such points of delicate, thematically 'superfluous' detail as the metrical pause arranged so that 'the sudden race of springs' can come with a rush (and the tactful use of thawed *springs* as a sign of *spring*), or the effect of stepping in 'tread', 'heard', '-ward' as the goddess climbs the stair from darkness to light, winter to spring.

The goddess is, of course, Proserpine; and that oblique reference to the underworld recalls the 'shallow hells' and 'pits' of the first section—the places spring and summer have been sadly banished to—just as the 'azure water hoisting' (as if by its own energy, like the plants' 'building', though it is in fact hoist*ed*) reminds us of the slightly sinister stagnant wells of the first section. So, too, the differing trees in each section help to unify a variety that is witty and sensuous, elegiac and celebratory, mocking and affirmative, progressive and accumulative.

The following poems by Richard Wilbur are recommended: *Castles and Distances, Marché aux Oiseaux, Year's End, The Terrace*, all in *Poems 1943–56*; *Shame, In the Smoking Car*, in *Contemporary American Poetry*, (Penguin 1962).

ISAAC ROSENBERG
Returning, we Hear the Larks
Chagrin

Commentary by Philip Hobsbaum

Returning, We Hear the Larks

Sombre the night is.
And though we have our lives, we know
What sinister threat lurks there.

Dragging these anguished limbs, we only know
5   This poison-blasted track opens on our camp—
On a little safe sleep.

But hark! joy—joy—strange joy.
Lo! heights of night ringing with unseen larks.
Music showering on our upturn'd list'ning faces.

10   Death could drop from the dark
As easily as song—
But song only dropped,
Like a blind man's dreams on the sand
By dangerous tides,
15   Like a girl's dark hair for she dreams no ruin lies there
Or her kisses where a serpent hides.

Chagrin

Caught still as Absalom,
Surely the air hangs
From the swayless cloud-boughs,
Like hair of Absalom
5   Caught and hanging still.

From the imagined weight
Of spaces in a sky
Of mute chagrin, my thoughts
Hang like branch-clung hair
10   To trunks of silence swung,
With the choked soul weighing down
Into thick emptiness.
Christ! end this hanging death,
For endlessness hangs therefrom.

15   Invisibly—branches break
      From invisible trees—
      The cloud-woods where we rush,
      Our eyes holding so much,
      Which we must ride dim ages round
20   Ere the hands (we dream) can touch,
      We ride, we ride, before the morning
      The secret roots of the sun to tread,
      And suddenly
      We are lifted of all we know
25   And hang from implacable boughs.

One of the things we have to remember in practical criticism is that anything we say can only be a selection of the things we feel. In writing criticism we are seeking to sort out what can be quite a complex pattern of responses. It would be possible in theory to define those responses qualitatively, but this would be of interest mainly to a psychologist, since it would tell a third party only about ourselves. In practice, therefore, we point to certain aspects of a poem in the hope that other readers will see those aspects too. But it must be remembered that other readers will most likely go on to isolate other aspects, those which exigencies of time of space have prevented us from discussing. Or, as is always possible, a given reader may not be able to see in the poem much of what we have pointed out. In such a case the fault may be with ourselves for not being sufficiently persuasive critics; with the reader, for being inattentive; or, as not infrequently happens, with the poem, for failing to make a decisive act of communication.

Another aspect of practical criticism—other, that is to say, than its selectivity—is its flexibility. Once we have accepted that it is impossible to number *all* the streaks upon the tulip, we can go on to decide in what order the few streaks we have time to number shall be presented. Some poems—those with a very straightforward plot—probably do demand a mode of criticism close to paraphrase; so that the critic selects his points, indeed, but selects them with regard to chronology. But most poems are more elliptical than that; especially most modern poems. And in such cases the critic would be well advised to seek out what has been called 'the experiential core'.

For even if a poem is of homogenous quality throughout, there are bound to be some lines which are more central than others; which 'give the clue', so to speak. The chronological process of numbering the points would not do much for *Returning, We Hear the Larks*. Paraphrase would make the poem seem like one about troops arrested by lark-song. It is about that, just as the literal component of any allegory needs to seem convincing on its own level. But in an allegory the literal narration does not exist for its own sake so much as an illustration of some larger truth. The same is true of the soldiers and the lark-song in *Returning, We Hear the Larks*.

The clue is given in the very last cadence:

> *Like a girl's dark hair for she dreams no ruin lies there,*
> *Or her kisses where a serpent lies.*

If this is simply a war poem, why do we have these lines? If it was simply a war poem the lines would be out of place, and therefore bad. But if we assume their relevance for the moment, what do we find when we read them?

Certainly there is a telling ambiguity in 'the girl's dark hair'. It may ruin her because it draws to her a false lover, or it may prove ruination to the lover. He must choose: behind the beauty may lie deceit and ultimately destruction.

The line 'like a girl's dark hair for she dreams no ruin lies there' has taken on a certain ambiguity. We are certain that the hair is destructive: we are not sure of whom. There is, too, the implication that, in either case, it is not the girl's fault—'she dreams no ruin lies there'; although even this is qualified—her belief is an illusion.

But the last line, 'Or her kisses where a serpent hides', is far less ambiguous. Here is a distinct implication of Eve, authoress of all our misfortunes. Indeed, and more sinisterly still, there is an *identification* of Eve with the serpent. (This is by no means an isolated instance: Empson has pointed out a similar effect in *Paradise Lost* in his *Milton and Bentley* essay.) We may enjoy her kisses, but they lead only to our wreck. One thinks of the medieval sermoniser: we are not so strong as Samson, so pious as David or so wise as Solomon, yet women undid all these three.

If we take the poem back a little now, we see that the girl's dreams are prepared for. She is not the only dreamer in this poem.

> *Like a blind man's dreams on the sand*
> *By dangerous tides . . .*

These are among the most haunting lines in the language. But why? There are four or five possibilities that are best held in some mental equipoise. (1) The blind man may be dreaming that he is no longer blind but walking on the sand; therefore his dream may have a very destructive conclusion. (2) The blind man may be dreaming that he is walking on the sand and may, in fact, actually be walking in his sleep; in which case he is in great physical danger. (3) The blind man may be preparing either his or someone else's destruction by dreaming it or ill-wishing it; as paranoiacs are said to set up the situations that destroy them. (4) The dreams themselves may be deadly, having an influence such as that of a curse or spell. (5) The two lines may be taken metaphorically. There are several possibilities in this last interpretation; the prime one, that a blind man walking among quicksands is about as safe from destruction as a boy ardently in love. Seen like this the last four lines fit together as a cohesive whole: a series of allegories for a fatal love affair. Let us read them forward a little.

> *Death could drop from the dark*
> *As easily as song—*
> *But song only dropped . . .*

In the confusion of experience we may easily make the wrong choice and so destroy ourselves. In this instance we made the right choice, but it was more good luck than good management. And the lines carry the further implication that even the good luck may have a destructive undercurrent. Now, with all this in our heads, we can begin to read the poem from the beginning.

Certainly the setting of the opening lines is based on war experience. For instance,

> *Dragging these anguished limbs, we only know*
> *This poison-blasted track opens on our camp . . .*

But in the light of the concluding lines, those we have just examined, we can say that the war experience is a referent for something larger—shall we hazard, the sheer unexpectedness both of joy and of anguish. The beginning is uncertain, though here uncertaintly seems to be a dramatic device.

> *Sombre the night is . . .*

Notice the inversion, so that the key word comes first and the line tails off on a weak word—'is'—lightly stressed.

> *And though we have our lives, we know*
> *What sinister threat lurks there.*

The gift of life is held on condition—'though we have our lives'—and all that is certain is uncertainty. What is behind the darkness? It is like asking what is behind a girl's mask—or her hair! All these soldiers want is an oasis in the desert—the 'poison-blasted track'—and they will find it if they are allowed to reach their camp and 'a little safe sleep'.

But they are not so allowed. They are halted. They could, as Rosenberg concedes, have been halted by shrapnel or by tracer bullets. But instead,

> *Lo! heights of night ringing with unseen larks.*
> *Music showering on our upturn'd list'ning faces.*

The first of these two lines superbly mimes the clamour of the larks—'heights of night ringing . . .' What Peter Porter has finely called 'the injustice of delight' does not come in any condition that would be recognised as 'a safe sleep'. On the contrary, Rosenberg has evidently taken pains to show the soldiers in a vulnerable attitude—'upturn'd list'ning faces'. One shudders to think what could have beaten down on those defenceless soldiers. 'Showering' could be true either of bullets or of song: either destruction or benefit could rain down, as the case may be. The condition is that the recipient be vulnerable. Only those who are vulnerable experience ecstasy; they also, sooner or later, come to fathom the abysses on which those ecstasies are based.

So that, in a way, Rosenberg is welcoming the condition of war: it sharpens one's senses and heightens the possibilities of life. By extension, Rosenberg is welcoming emotional experience, the chance of the girl's dark hair and her kisses balanced by the equal chance of the dangerous tides, the ruin, the serpent. The suburban householder counsels 'take care'. But the poet ripostes 'live dangerously'. (Rosenberg was killed on 1 April 1918.)

But the poem is not 'simply' about the dangers of love, any more than it is 'simply' about the ecstasies of war. It includes these possibilities, and many more, in a dramatic statement, properly an enactment, of an attitude we can only call 'walking the knife-edge of experience'.

> *Though we have our lives, we know*
> *What sinister threat lurks there.*

Because of this threat we are aware of our lives; as only a man who has been threatened with blindness can truly value the vestiges of vision that remain to him.

Rosenberg approaches this concept elliptically, allowing it to suggest itself through the familiar images of war. But we can now see why Siegfried Sassoon refused to call him a war poet. Something larger even than that immediate scene was going on in Rosenberg's poems. And to bring this out perhaps we should turn to a poem which, so far as I know, has never been anthologised or commented upon, though it is one of Rosenberg's finest. It has at first sight nothing to do with war.

In *Chagrin* the temptation is to focus upon the obvious leading theme—Absalom hung by his abundant hair from the bough. But, once more, this is not the centre of the poem. We should turn the poem about to discover what, after all, is the central situation. I think we shall find it in these lines—

> From the imagined weight
> Of spaces in a sky
> Of mute chagrin, my thoughts
> Hang like branch-clung hair . . .

It is as though the protagonist of the poem were staring fixedly at a particular cloudscape—

> Surely the air hangs
> From the swayless cloud-boughs . . .

In what the psychiatrists call a state of emotional shock, the patient tends to stare fixedly at one particular sector of his visual range. This is true, also, of depressives: the attempt to get through to them is often baulked, I understand, by the fixity of their attention elsewhere. Something similar is done by that pernicious drug LSD. Artists, especially painters, often take it because it compels them to give obsessive attention to an object—a milk-bottle? a lamp?—which hitherto had been a matter of passing notice. And six students in California, hooked on acid, went blind trying to outstare the sun. Something like this state—for which chagrin is the mildest possible name—seems to me what Rosenberg is depicting here.

Having found the experiential core, we can once more begin to read the poem forwards.

> Caught still as Absalom
> Surely the air hangs
> From the swayless cloud-boughs,
> Like hair of Absalom
> Caught and hanging still.

Notice how careful Rosenberg is to keep the Absalom myth in check in case it runs away with the whole poem. It would have been all too easy to make the scene as realistically particular as the 'poison-blasted track' of Returning, We Hear the Larks. Instead, Absalom comes in for the first time as a simile: we begin with a cloudscape, and the clouds are compared with boughs from which depends the air—a subdued pun here—'like hair of Absalom'. The description, then, is not simply of Absalom hanging by his hair, nor even of air motionless beneath the clouds. Rather it is an evocation of stasis, and the clouds and the hair of Absalom are two out of many possible examples of this.

However, although Absalom is introduced as simile rather than as direct narrative, he certainly underpins the next section.

> ... *my thoughts*
> *Hang like branch-clung hair*
> *To trunks of silence swung,*
> *With the choked soul weighing down*
> *Into thick emptiness* ...

The stasis is here seen to be an emotional one—let us say, the condition of shock after a psychologically wounding experience. The hair or (the pun is still active) *air* is a simulacrum of the thoughts of the man imagining the former, watching the latter. One reason for his focusing in dream and in reality upon such objects is because they empathise with the fixity of his mood. 'Branch-clung hair' gives us, with fascinating insight, a glimpse into the tangle of conflicting emotions that has produced the stasis. Nothing could be much more entangled than 'branch-clung hair'. One cannot tell whether the hair is clinging to the branch or vice versa, and there are appalling secondary meanings, such as the wife clinging to her husband (especially when he goes off to war) or the phrase about clinging to life. The stasis is made more awful by the suggestion of movement—'to trunks of silence swung'—and the nothingness upon which the 'choked soul' depends. Just as the air depends, but only from the clouds, and the boughs sustaining Absalom are described as clouds, so here the branches—compared with 'spaces in the sky'—relate only to a trunk of silence. There is nothing healthy in this immobility at all. The soul is in a tensed position between the mute chagrin of the sky and the thick emptiness below.

> *Christ! end this hanging death,*
> *For endlessness hangs therefrom.*

Perhaps the ultimate chagrin was that of Christ, hanging on the cross—'my God, my God, why hast thou forsaken me?' Therefore it is appropriate that he be implored to end this stasis—nothing can break it from within—since he alone could truly understand it.

But there is no way out of a malaise like this except—as Freud said—by understanding it. So in order to understand his mood the protagonist looks back a little at what occasioned it. The effect is of the view upon which he is fixated disintegrating before his puzzled eyes.

> *Invisibly—branches break*
> *From invisible trees . . .*

Though even this mirrors his inward anguish: it is *invisible* branches that break. And what do we see? The hope of our youth, the egotism of adolescence, the hubris of the young male—

> *The cloud-woods where we rush,*
> *Our eyes holding so much,*
> *Which we must ride dim ages round*
> *Ere the hands (we dream) can touch . . .*

Though there is a struggle, the youth (or former self) is sure it can be surmounted. Time ('dim ages') is nothing; neither is difficulty ('cloud woods'). We'll rush at them!

> *We ride, we ride, before the morning*
> *The secret roots of the sun to tread . . .*

The rhythm, the insouciance, all give promise of a reversal: this is pinpointed by the ironic inflation of the lines, especially the repetition of 'we ride'. There is also more than a suggestion of criticism, of the older man for his former self. Where, after all, are we to 'tread' the 'secret roots of the sun'? It is as though no one was worthy of sex—once more, 'the injustice of delight'—and so the protagonist shares at once the guilt so many human animals have about intercourse and also risk the possibilities (as in *Returning, We Hear the Larks*) of the abyss. And even in tracing the cause of his malaise—notice the whole section is in the present tense—the protagonist finds himself back in it again. With a convulsive kick the line breaks off short—

> *And suddenly*
> *We are lifted of all we know*
> *And hang from implacable boughs.*

All the living, breathing, human world is left behind—'we are lifted of all we know'—in this unalterable depression of the spirits.

One undercurrent so far unremarked is a clue which Rosenberg left—a clue which limits the poem to one particular kind of emotional shock. The clue is in these lines:

> *Our eyes holding so much*
> *Which we must ride dim ages round*
> *Ere the hands (we dream) can touch.*

We have already seen what Rosenberg thought of dreams. Here we have a distinct insight into what he was dreaming about. 'Our eyes holding so much'—surely this the famous and archetypal locked eyebeam of two lovers? or possibly the young man contemplating his goal. 'Ere the hands (we dream) can touch'—is this not the belief so many youngsters have that love can be struggled for, that the pains one goes through *deserve* the final reward, of one's loved one? This romantic misapprehension (Lawrence knew far better) has brought about great unhappiness and a vast crop of mostly Petrarchan love poems. And it seems to me that its savage disappointment here is at the core of this remarkable poem.

It would be even more remarkable a poem if Rosenberg had not chosen to make the underpinning so apparent. This is true, also, of *Returning, We Hear the Larks*. In the latter poem the possibility of a meaning relating to love is only one of many, but the possibilities are fined down throughout the poem, even to the ambiguity of the penultimate line until we are left with the tragic last statement—'her kisses where a serpent lies'. In *Chagrin* the possibilities are held much more skilfully in equipoise except for that moment when the agony breaks through—'ere the hands . . .'

Skill, subtlety—these seem to be the prime characteristics of

Rosenberg's poetry. It is strange that they have not more clearly been brought out in critical commentary. So far the most valuable essay to have been written on Rosenberg is D. W. Harding's early piece in *Scrutiny*; this stresses mainly the language of the poems.*
But perhaps the most extraordinary tribute to Rosenberg is his influence over poets of my own generation, particularly Peter Redgrove, Ted Hughes and Jon Silkin. Certainly there is much yet to be learned from Rosenberg's free plasm of verse which never degenerates into prose, his masterly use of association, his astonishingly original diction. Apart from the two poems just discussed, *Break of Day in the Trenches*, *Louse Hunting*, *Daughters of War*, *God*, *Moses* and *Dead Man's Dump* seem to me masterpieces—especially the last two.

But what strikes me as being the prime characteristic of Rosenberg, and what I have tried to bring out in my analysis of these two poems, is his extraordinary mastery of plot. The elliptical unfolding can often tell us more than a direct statement, simply because it tells us several related things at once. On this sector I have concentrated my criticism. There are many ways of talking about Rosenberg's poems other than this thematic way, but consideration of theme seemed most relevant to my present purpose. I hope it leads readers into considering other aspects of his work, and some young writers, perhaps, into learning from him.

* It appears also in D. W. Harding, *Experience into Words*, Chatto & Windus, 1963.

HUGH MACDIARMID
First Hymn to Lenin
By Wauchopeside

Commentary by David Craig

First Hymn to Lenin

(To Prince D. S. Mirsky)

Few even o the criminals, cravens, and fools
Wha's voices vilify a man they ken
They've cause to fear and are unfit to judge
As they're to stem his influence again
5   But in the hollows where their hearts should be
                Foresee your victory.

Churchills, Locker-Lampsons, Beaverbrooks'll be
In history's perspective less to you
(And them!) than the centurions to Christ
10   Of whom, as you, at least this muckle's true
    —'Tho pairtly wrang he cam to richt amang's
                Faur greater wrangs.'

Christ's cited no by chance or juist because
You mark the greatest turnin-point since him
15   But that your main redress has lain where he's
Least use—fulfillin his sayin lang kept dim
That whasae followed him things o like natur
                Ud dae—and greater!

Certes nae ither if no you's dune this.
20   It maitters little. What you've dune's the thing,
No hoo't compares, corrects, or complements
The work o Christ that's taen owre lang to bring
Sic a successor to keep the reference back
                Natural to mak.

25   Great things hae aye taen great men in the past
In some proportion to the work they did,
But you alane to what you've dune are nocht
Even as the pooers to greater ends are hid
In what's ca'd God, or in the common man,
30   Withoot your plan.

Descendant o the unkent bards wha made
Sangs peerless through a' post-anonymous days,
I glimpse again in you that mightier pooer

Than fashes wi the laurels and the bays
35   But kens that it is shared by ilka man
                    Since time began.

Great things, great men—but at faur greater's cost!
If first things first had had their richtfu sway
Life and Thocht's misused pooer might hae been ane
40   For a' men's benefit—as still they may
Noo that through you this mair than elemental force
                    Has fund a clearer course.

Christ said: 'Save ye become as bairns again.'
Bairnly eneuch the feck o us hae been!
45   Your work needs men; and its worst foes are juist
The traitors wha through a' history hae gien
The dope that's gard the mass o folk pay heed
                    And bide bairns indeed.

As necessary, and insignificant, as death
50   Wi a' its agonies in the cosmos still
The Cheka's horrors are in their degree;
And'll end suner! What maitters't wha we kill
To lessen that foulest murder that deprives
                    Maist men o real lives!

55   For now in the flower and iron of the truth
To you we turn, and turn in vain nae mair:
Ilka fool has folly eneuch for sadness
But at last we are wise and wi laughter tear
The veil of being, and are face to face
60   Wi the human race.

Here lies your secret, O Lenin—yours and oors,
No in the majority will that accepts the result
But in the real will that bides its time and kens
The benmaist resolve is the pooer in which we exult
Since naebody's willingly deprived o the good;
                    And, least o a', the crood!

2. ken know; 34. fashes bothers; 44. feck majority; 47. gard made; 48. bide stay;
64. benmaist inmost

37

By Wauchopeside

Thrawn water? Aye, owre thrawn to be aye thrawn!
I hae my wagtails like the Wauchope tae,
Birds fu o fechtin spirit, and o fun,
That whiles jig in the air in lichtsome play
5   Like glass-bas on a fountain, syne stand still
Save for a quiver, shoot up an inch or twa, fa back
Like a swarm o winter-gnats, or are tost aside
        By their inclination's kittle loup
         To balance efter hauf a coup.
10 There's mair in birds than men hae faddomed yet.
Tho maist churn oot the stock sangs o their kind
There's aiblins genius here and there, and aince
'Mang whitebeams, hollies, siller birks—
        The tree o licht—
15   I mind

I used to hear a blackie mony a nicht
Singin awa t'an unconscionable oor
Wi nocht but the water keepin't company
(Or nocht that ony human ear could hear).
20 —And wondered if the blackie heard it either
Or cared whether it was singin tae or no!
O there's nae sayin what my verses awn
To memories like these. Hae I come back
To find oot? Or to borrow mair? Or see
25 Their helpless puirness to what gard them be?
        Late sang the blackie but it stopt at last.
        The river still gaed singin past.

O there's nae sayin what my verses awn
To memories, or my memories to me.
30 But ae thing's certain: even as things stand
I could vary them in coontless ways and gie
Wauchope a new course in the minds o men,
The blackie gowden feathers, and the like,
And yet no cease to be dependent on

35   *The things o Nature, and create instead*
         Oot o my ain heid
         Or get ootside the range
         O trivial change
   Into that cataclysmic country which
40   *Natheless a' men inhabit—and enrich.*

   For civilisation in its struggle up
   Has mair than seasonal changes o ideas,
   Glidin through periods o flooers and fruit,
   Winter and Spring again; to cope wi these
45   *Is difficult eneuch to tax the patience*
   O Methuselah himsel—but transformations,
   Yont physical and mental habits, symbols, rites
   That mak sic changes nane, are aye gaen on,
   Revolutions in the dynasty o live ideals
50   *—The stuff wi which alane true poetry deals.*
   Wagtail or water winna help me here
   (That's clearer than Wauchope at its clearest's clear!),
   Where the life o a million years is seen
   Like a louch look in a lass's een.

1. Thrawn stubborn, *aye* always; *5. syne* then; *8. kittle* unpredictable, *loup* jump; *9. coup* tumble; *12. aiblins* maybe; *54. louch* downcast

In reprinting these two poems I have slightly altered the spelling of the Scots words. The usual practice with British printers has been to put apostrophes where the Scots spelling differs from the English—ha'e for have, singin' for singing, and so on. But this suggests that the Scots is an erroneous form, which misses out letters that should be there. The fact is that Scots and English are cognate, both of them being derived from the older language of the British Isles. I have therefore left in the apostrophes only where it was necessary to distinguish the word from another one, e.g. a' for all and ca'd for called.

These poems by a Scotsman are in a language so close to commoner forms of 'English' that readers unused to Scots are not likely to make heavy weather of it unless they are already minded to do so. The fourteen words used by MacDiarmid that are so unlike any current English ones as to be obscure are translated in footnotes. In the case of all others that are very like their English counterparts—'ither' for 'other', 'maist' for 'most', 'hauf' for 'half', and so on—

readers will probably find that if they are alert enough to be responding to the poetry, the meaning of the Scots, too, will be carrying across with little extra effort. It also helps if the poems are read aloud: many a word that may seem veiled in the strangeness of the 'foreign' spelling will turn out to echo closely its English counterpart once it is heard spoken.

In any case you should read aloud every poem that you spend time on at all, for this is the most direct and natural way into the full effect of the words. It has often been noticed that a writer's distinctive way of using words springs partly from the characteristic pace and rhythm of his own mental workings and even his voice. Hence the saying, 'Style is the man'. From this it follows that if you reconvert the language of a poem into speech, you will be getting its effect more fully than if you allowed it to remain on the page. I say its 'effect' rather than its meaning, because effect is more than meaning. Meaning is basically what the words define; but we need also to catch and consider the way in which the poet is addressing whoever he imagines is listening: is he transmitting at full voice to a crowd, or even a whole nation? is he entertaining a familiar circle? is he confiding in one person close to him? or thinking aloud? or some blend of these? When we read a poem we should find its wavelength, by trying to arrive at the pace, volume, rhythm, and tone of voice that seems to suit it best. For example, at the start of *By Wauchopeside* there is a question: 'Thrawn water? Aye . . .' Doesn't this sound as though the poet had an imaginary addressee in mind: 'Thrawn did you say? Yes indeed . . .'? Thus right away the relaxed musing-aloud tone is set, and with it the feeling of a man plumbing something he has long been familiar with but never wholly understood. Contrast with this the considered assertion with which the *Hymn to Lenin* opens. If the reader alerts himself in this way, he will be able to enter into the poem with a fullness difficult to manage otherwise.

If the *Hymn* begins by asserting an opinion and *Wauchopeside* by thinking aloud, these poems evidently go in for *thought*. We can see as they unfold that they are concerned not so much to evoke a mood, a passion, or an atmosphere as to develop arguments, albeit in lyrical form. In the *Hymn* there are ideas about two particularly influential men, Lenin and Jesus, and both have been much written about in the form of what is most usually called 'thought'—theology, political theory and controversy, and so on: lines 43–8 and 61–6 borrow ideas and even phrases from Marx's *Capital*, his essay on Hegel's *Philosophy of Right*, and Lenin's article on 'Socialism and Religion'. In *Wauchopeside* there are ideas about poetry and about civilisation, and both have been much discussed by critics and philosophers. MacDiarmid never fully defines 'civilisation' or the relation between memories and poetic images, yet the poem is about these and comes at them from many angles; just as the *Hymn* never fully defines the 'contribution' of Lenin or Jesus, nor proves that outstanding individuals are channels for inevitable historical processes, yet these are the notions that keep reappearing and becoming more concrete bit by bit. This implies both that such poetry overlaps with philosophy, etc, and that it is a different way of using language. A poet who sets out to write, lyrically, about the sources of his own imagery or about the course of history will of course know roughly what he thinks about them, he will already have followed out some relevant trains of thought. But he is reaching us through distinctively artistic means: for example, highly personal images, the physical properties of words as well as their dictionary meanings, and so on. His poem will to some extent take shape as he writes: links between main thoughts, brand-new minor thoughts and so on will occur to him as he writes; they will not have been fully mapped beforehand as they would by a writer in a systematic form. Even the need to find a rhyme may deflect—that is, may prompt—a poet to express meanings that otherwise would have stayed hidden somwhere in his mind.

So we are not to expect from poetry, however philosophical, the rigorously sequential logic, the definite conclusions, that belong in an essay by David Hume or Marx or A. J. Ayer. This is not an excuse for talking nonsense. What it implies, among other things, is that the signs in poetry of a swerve into dishonesty or an ill-grounded suggestion will be different from the inaccuracy or false logic that are among the signs of bad argument in the systematic kinds of writing. For example, verse 9 of the *Hymn* does something disgusting that had better be discussed at once: it justifies the police tyranny—the imprisonment without trial, slavery, and judicial murder—that increasingly disfigured the Soviet Union in the 'thirties and 'forties. The question is whether all we can do is object to the opinion of Stalinism expressed in the poem or whether we can find in the wording of that verse false notes, flat or careless wording, and so on which might be the signs of an idea being blustered at us rather than fully ripened by the poet before he offered it. It would surely be better if the point could be settled by such critical means rather than allowed to move over into an area of controversy which is important in itself but impossible to handle satisfactorily inside a discussion whose first duty is to literature.

If, then, we remain open to the poem as poetry and if we also try it aloud and let its rhythm and flow invade our minds, I believe we will sense a steady onward movement down the page, as though of an unwavering voice that can go on for long without taking breath. The pauses are in fact few: it is extraordinary that although the verse is a long and regular one and hardly varies, each of the first three verses is a complete sentence, altogether eight of the eleven are like that, and the first verse in particular pauses very little, at those commas in the first line. The train of thought unfolds, without strain or constriction, inside a form whose sustained pattern is a pleasure in itself. The effect is like that of a long melody in a symphony by Dvořák or a folk-style song by Ewan MacColl. It means that the poetry appeals to us by a kind of large steady music which is at the same time the style or voice of intellectual certitude. The justifiability of what the poet is being certain about is not the point here, although if the content of the poem went clean against our own views (for example, if it were a hymn to Hitler) probably no style could save it. The point is that MacDiarmid, by fixing his thoughts on Lenin, has enabled himself to take a long view of history and consider human development in its entirety. He has built his poem out of solid general statements: the question is whether the wording is concrete or subtle enough to save them from coming out as groundless abstractions. For example (line 29), neither 'God' nor 'the common man' is a strikingly precise notion: both are in danger of acting as rallying points for automatic support, or for that matter automatic scepticism. But the effect of linking them, as alternative types of life-as-a-whole, is to give more meaning to each: each is being seen as, in its own epoch, the final measure of value. Again (line 39), it might seem merely utopian to suppose that 'misused life and thought' could ever have 'acted together for all men's good'. But at least this large supposition is at once qualified by the conditional 'may' and by 'still' with its implied 'perhaps, some day . . .'.

The style of the poem, then, is generally 'high', weighty: for example, many lines use the same word both before and after the natural break or caesura, which gives them a symmetrical structure, like an arch. But it seems to me that this style is checked often enough to put a brake on any heady idealism that might run away with it (although I can see that, if the poem is open to question, it is in this way). The main checking devices seem to be the interruptions, usually colloquial; the short line that ends each verse; and the many terms from logic that in places give the poem a feel quite different from the 'musical' one already emphasised. The colloquial remarks alter any image we might be forming of the poet as an exalted orator. The first verse, especially if is turned into English (which can easily be done), might seem a bit old-fashioned, in diction, phrasing, and metre. But this is broken in upon by the final phrase of verse 3 (line 18), with its effect of chipping in almost cheekily to cap Jesus's prophecy. The convinced finality of line 19 is followed at once by the abrupt, unceremonious 'It maitters little. What you've dune's the thing', spoken as though to a comrade near at hand, not to a historical personage across the years.

Secondly, if each verse had moved to a resounding close, which might well have been the effect if the last line had been long, we might suspect that an exalted rhetoric was taking over and trying to hypnotise us into going along with it. But the short lines both break the 'music' and clinch stages in the argument. Their rhyming with the preceding line helps to tap them home, but of course it is the words and their meanings that matter most, and it is worth running your eye down those eleven final lines to see what the verbal features are that contribute to the effect of a nail squarely hit.

Thirdly, the many 'large' phrases—'history's perspective', 'the greatest turning-point', 'Descendants o the unkent bards', 'the veil of being'—are balanced, their booming effect is damped, by the logical terms which show an alert intellect taking care to be precise even about its own favourite brain-children. 'Cited' and 'reference back' are careful, even pedantic terms. At the end of the second verse it is implied that Lenin is at least 'partly wrong'. At the start of the third verse the poem's own technique of setting up an ideal type is scrutinised, and in the fourth various ways of making the Lenin/Jesus parallel too close are rebutted in general terms. Although the poem is called a hymn, and the mode is sometimes invocation, the style is often that of argument: possibilities are put up and contradicted; sweeping statements are qualified; terms used are later turned back on and perhaps half withdrawn.

Such are the touches that give the large generalities their convincing feel—if it is agreed that this convincingness does come about. Readers may want to ask whether there is enough of the stuff of Lenin's life and the Russian situation in the poem. If the two words 'Cheka' and 'Lenin' were not there, could we tell to whom it was addressed? The general degree of abstraction, as in lines like 'If first things first had had their richtfu sway', is usually a danger sign in literature; has MacDiarmid got away with it at least for as long as this poem lasts? Such questions must be asked, although any one group may well have to agree to differ on their answers.

By Wauchopeside is recognisably by the same poet: different readers would probably suggest different grounds for such a judgment, but for me it is again that quality of fairly complicated, fairly abstract thought unfolding inside a handsome lyric form. And again this is managed by the unwinding of lengthy sentences that stretch across the lines: I rather think—and it could be checked, in the first place by using the other poems in this book—that the sentence lengths are unusually varied. Once again there is a mixture of involved thoughts and 'spontaneous' interruptions or asides.

The differences between *By Wauchopeside* and the *Hymn* are as necessary to notice, for it is one sign of a remarkable writer that he is always recognisably himself yet can get an inexhaustible variety of suggestions from the area of meaning and expression that he has made his own. Although *By Wauchopeside* has elements of impersonal generalisation, by comparison with the *Hymn* it is introspective: the first-person singular is common in it, rare in the *Hymn*; there are more question-marks than exclamation-marks (again contrast the *Hymn*), the questions they mark are short but deep-reaching, and they are put mainly to himself. In short he is thinking aloud. Hence it follows a more wayward, less sequential course than the *Hymn*, it takes longer to reach the core of its subject, and it does so by intuitive jumps or links: it is worth studying the associations by which the poet gets from river to birds to his own creative processes. Indeed much of this 'waywardness' shows at a glance, in the shape of the poem, which of course is determined by the length of the lines. Their variety, from the full five-stress line to nearly the shortest possible, springs from the natural flow and recoil of the poet's mental impulses, not from fitting words into a given pattern. That place at the close of verse 1 where the variation is greatest is specially worth dwelling on: the precise frame of mind or inner 'set' that it evokes should reveal itself fully if the reader tries it aloud until he finds the pace and volume of reading that feel right.

Once the poet has reached the core of his subject, the long sentences start to unfold—still longer than those in the *Hymn*. Notice that they have a genuine, close-knit logic: they have not been made, for the most part, by tacking on phrases in apposition, adding one principal clause to another punctuated by commas that amount to full-stops, or anything like that. In the sentence (line 30) that starts 'But ae thing's certain', or the sentence (line 41) that starts 'For civilisation', the items linked are genuinely necessary to each other and very few could be cut without damaging the train of thought. The best way into such trains of thought is to hold onto the syntax—make sure you are seeing what is the subject of each clause, what an indefinite 'it' or 'them' refers to, and so on, and then you gain in two ways. You get a sense of being present at the very forming of the thoughts; and you grasp what exactly is being said and what discarded, what are the ins and outs of the matter, and especially what seemingly or partly contradictory notions are being balanced together in the third and fourth verses.

There we have a main characteristic of poetry that expresses thoughts: it does go into ideas but it hardly seeks to prove them or come up with definitions of them that logically could not be faulted. For example, there is no distinct definition (in verse 4) of 'live ideals', these entities that evidently go beyond the more shortlived kinds of 'mental habits'. Yet do we feel that we are being fobbed off with flimsy abstractions? or do we feel that we have been given access to a mind in the act of introspecting upon itself as it turns over ideas deep-seated in it? Again, we would not expect to get from philosophy or other formal types of thinking a sense of the person's situation as he did the thinking (although there are important exceptions, e.g. the dialogues of Socrates as told by Plato, the parables of Jesus as told by the apostles). But in the poem this is of the essence. The situation beside the River Wauchope is not a backdrop or surface colouring. The river itself is everywhere amongst the thoughts. Notice how its movements, its course, its animals and plants, its own transparent quality come into every verse, first as the starting-point or original subject, then as a source of symbols for the main theme and for further imaginative sugges-tions to which the poet's musing leads him. This is what knits the thing together until we feel we have undergone a whole experience, from the most conscious (formal thinking, deliberate recall, direct speech) to the deeper layers (the swarming up of memories which then move the poet to think out why they matter to him). Above all, this tissue of experience unfolds naturally: the poet is so at home in this piece of country and the frame of mind that goes with it that he can chat to it in homely phrases. Probably it is these ways of staying close to the experience that help the poem to avoid the dubious, and at one point frankly unacceptable, kinds of thing that detract from the *Hymn*. To my ear only one line in *By Wauchopeside*— 'The stuff wi which alane true poetry deals'— has the flatness of unleavened generality, whereas most readers might agree on finding several such in the *Hymn*.

In your reading you must have found that phrases and lines stay unbidden in the memory, and not only for their meaning, their point, but also for how they go, like a phrase of music that enters the mind irresistibly. Sometimes such a piece can be recognised right away, by the unerring way in which one word is felt to move into place after another. Such a point comes for me in the tenth verse of the *Hymn*: it 'lifts' with the echoing open vowels of 'now in the flower' and the sensuous imagery (unique in the poem) of 'flower and iron', breaks into the gruff disclaimer of 'Ilka fool . . .', then lifts again with the large image of 'The veil of being' and the finality of the last clause. In *By Wauchopeside*, at the close of the second verse, we are still expecting questions, but then comes that

46

couplet: the long even breath or motion of 'Late sang the blackie but it stopt at last'—stop—a shorter but again continuous line—stop. And this mixture of onflow and pause enacts what the words are saying. So all the verbal means fuse to create a moment of absorption—the whole being intent at a juncture where only one thing is stirring. These lines hit me when I first read them in 1966, and have never left me, but it was not until just now that I tried to find out how they worked. That is the use of analysis: it remains so much wearisome fiddling, done to score academic points, unless one's original experience of the work has been powerful enough to come alive again at each rereading. This does not mean that we have to *wait* for powerful experiences. They can be sought out, especially from authors we have reason to think are fine. But we must enter into each work, not with expectations too ready-made, but rather with the relaxed readiness of a ballerina between dances.

THOMAS HARDY
Overlooking the River Stour
On Sturminster Foot-Bridge
The Sheep Boy

Commentary by T. R. Barnes

Overlooking the River Stour

The swallows flew in the curves of an eight
    Above the river-gleam
    In the wet June's last beam:
Like little crossbows animate
5   The swallows flew in the curves of an eight
    Above the river-gleam.

Planing up shavings of crystal spray
    A moor-hen darted out
    From the bank thereabout,
10 And through the stream-shine ripped his way,
Planing up shavings of crystal spray
    A moor-hen darted out.

Closed were the kingcups; and the mead
    Dripped in monotonous green,
15   Though the day's morning sheen
Had shown it golden and honeybee'd;
Closed were the kingcups; and the mead
    Dripped in monotonous green.

And never I turned my head, alack,
20   While these things met my gaze
    Through the pane's drop-drenched glaze,
To see the more behind my back. . . .
O never I turned, but let, alack,
    These less things hold my gaze.'

On Sturminster Foot-bridge

Onomatopoeic

Reticulations creep upon the slack stream's face
    When the wind skims irritably past,
The current clucks smartly into each hollow place
That years of flood have scrabbled in the pier's sodden base;
5   The floating-lily leaves rot fast.

On a roof stand the swallows ranged in wistful waiting rows,
Till they arrow off and drop like stones
Among the eyot-withies at whose foot the river flows:
And beneath the roof is she who in the dark world shows
10   As a lattice-gleam when midnight moans.

The Sheep Boy

A yawning, sunned concave
Of purple, spread as an ocean wave
Entroughed on a morning of swell and sway
After a night when wind-fiends have been heard to rave:
5   Thus was the Heath called 'Draäts' on an August day.
Suddenly there intunes a hum:
This side, that side, it seems to come.
From the purple in myriads rise the bees
With consternation mid their rapt employ.
10   So headstrongly each speeds him past, and flies,
As to strike the face of the Shepherd-boy.
Awhile he waits, and wonders what they mean;
Till none is left upon the shagged demesne.

To learn what ails, the sheep-boy looks around;
15   Behind him, out of the sea in swirls
Flexuous and solid, clammy vapour-curls
Are rolling over Pokeswell Hills to the inland ground,
Into the heath they sail,
And travel up the vale
20   Like the moving pillar of cloud raised by the Israelite:
In a trice the lonely sheep-boy seen so late ago,
Draäts-Hollow in gorgeous blow,
And Kite-Hill's regal glow,
Are viewless-folded into those creeping scrolls of white.

Hardy's verse is not often melliflous or sonorous or suave. Though
he obviously derives from Romantic and Victorian traditions, and
adapts their forms to his personal needs, there is a toughness about

him, a desire to get things exactly right, to put down the truth just as he saw it even at the expense of what was felt by his fellows to be truly poetic, which sets him apart from other poets of his time. He wrote on a very wide range of themes, and in the three short poems we are going to discuss he can be seen to be working in the tradition of English nature poetry, to which he brings not only acuteness of observation and an eye for detail—qualities he shares with other poets—but also a kind of harsh honesty. The scene is set down as it appears before him, and is not edited in the interests of picturesqueness or conventional beauty.

The poems also illustrate the extraordinary variety of his metrical patterns—we have only to flick over the leaves of the *Collected Poems* to see that almost every set of verses has a different shape. We shall examine in some detail the form of each of them because this will help us to hear how they should 'go', to respond to their rhythms, to grasp their uniqueness, and to understand how their sound and movement relate to their sense—how, indeed these qualities are an inextricable part of that sense. We are therefore trying to extricate the inextricable, and such effort may well appear clumsy, pedantic and irrelevant. Poetry is, after all, for enjoyment; pleasure, said Wordsworth, is its great principle. The critic's only excuse must be that he is trying, however maladroitly, to evoke that pleasure where it does not exist, or to increase it where it does.

The first poem, *Overlooking the River Stour*, has the tightest pattern. In each stanza (except for tiny but significant changes in the last, to which we will return later) the first two and the last two lines are the same. This is a sort of ritual repetition which makes us feel the poem to be a chant or incantation, and lends weight and significance to the central 'monotonous'. Each six-line stanza is made up of two interlocking triple patterns. The long and short lines alternate *a bb aa b* and the rhymes move in the same way. The metrical arrangement looks simple, being made up of lines of three or four stresses, but it is subtly complicated by the mixture— characteristic of Hardy—of triple and duple rhythms, which the poet adapts to minute shifts of sense and feeling.

Three-quarters of the poem is about the things that met the poet's gaze. The phrase implies a certain passivity on his part; as he idly stares scenes and events impinge on his consciousness; they meet him, they have as much, perhaps more, life than he has, at this moment. Both scenes and events are vividly called before us, for there is no passivity in them; every creature, every object, is doing something. We can feel in the first line how the swallows move, for the triple rhythms—'in the curve of an eight'—(you can call them anapaests if you like) embody their rise and fall; the image of the 'little crossbows', odd, arresting and exact, makes us see the units that move. The light is fading. We do not so much see the river as become aware of it by reflection, by its gleam; and in the third line the row of monosyllables—'wet June's last beam' demand strong and equal stresses, bringing home to us the lingering twilight, the long-drawn-out death of the day. 'Gleam' and 'beam' are here nouns, but they can also be verbs and seem here to carry with them a sense of dim and fugitive being.

After the swallows, the moor-hen. Everyone must feel the energy, the happy visual precision, the bare unpoetic truth, of 'Planing up shavings of crystal spray', and how the falling triple rhythms fit the force of the bird which is not in free flight, but pressing its body over the water. (We have here in fact a kind of rhythmical inversion of the line about the swallows.) The verb 'rips' carries on the planing image—a plane rips shavings off wood—and the repeated r's in 'through', 'stream' and 'ripped' all reinforce the effect. The vague 'thereabout' might seem a piece of clumsiness, just a word put in to fill up a rhyme, but its vagueness fits the moor-hen perfectly. She has a habit of moving concealed along the water's edge and darting out where least expected.

The third stanza returns to the wet, sad June, to the static setting of the poem. 'Closed' stands strongly at the beginning of its first and penultimate lines. The flower which might have added colour to the 'monotonous green' is closed, as the day is closing. We pause after 'kingcups', and the next sense-group runs on. 'Dripped', like 'closed', stands heavily at the beginning of a line, with an emphasis reinforced by the run-on, and the effort we have to make when we pronounce the terminal and initial d's (there is a related effect in 'drop-drenched') and the mechanical precision with which the spoken and metrical stresses coincide when we say 'in monotonous green' all seem to embody the dreariness of the scene. Morning, 'golden and honey-bee'd' (a characteristic Hardy coinage) makes a moving contrast with the gloomy evening a contrast which prepares for, and gives poignancy to, the end of the poem.

The last stanza brings in the poet-observer, and the drama that he then ignored, but now knows he should have played a part in. We realise, with a sudden shock, two dimensions of time: one in which the scene was observed, and later when the poem was written. We are told nothing precise, and we feel the poem would be less powerful if we were. The tiniest hints suffice to convey the situation, and Hardy is able to make them do this because of the way he exploits the poem's pattern. The slightest disturbance of its tight symmetry takes on an immense significance. First, the negative: 'And never I turned my head'. All the other statements are positive—the swallows flew, the moor-hen darted, the kingcups were closed, the mead dripped, but the poet did *not* turn his head, and we feel this denial the more because of the placing of 'never' before the verb.

Some may feel the literary archaic 'alack' to be a weakness, but when we read Hardy we must take his diction as we find it. Unlike some poets, he seems to have had no theories on this subject— crossbows, planes and shavings are scarcely conventional poetic objects, but he makes them work. It is true, however, that at moments of heightened sentiment he does sometimes tend to use a hackneyed rhetoric; but I would not think that 'alack' so spoils this stanza. 'Glaze' is interesting. It fits the passivity already noted, of the things meeting his gaze; it bears suggestions of a glazed eye, and of the whole scene being covered by a kind of transparent envelope, of nature, as it were, in aspic; and this, we realise now, is how it is in truth fixed in the poet's memory, by association with a bitterly regretted moment in his life, the moment which makes up what we have called the drama of the poem, when 'The more', the beloved person, to whom he should have been but was not attending, remained behind him unseen, unthought of. The minute changes continue to rivet the situation to our minds. 'And' becomes the charged, emotive 'O'; the verb 'let' appears, suspended, and we fall to the last line, where we must, I think, feel the series of mono-syllables to be all equally, and all gravely, stressed. 'Less' springs out in poignant contrast to 'more'; 'things' stands for the whole substance of the first three verses; 'hold' closes the resonance

54

suspended in 'let', and 'my gaze' returns us to the poet's central, mistaken attitude. So the tiny moving anecdote is completed.

There is a similar situation in *On Sturminster Foot-bridge*, in so far as the description of a natural scene is rounded off with an allusion to a person, in this case clearly a 'she'; but we somehow do not feel as concerned about this as we do about the ending of the first poem. Its final phrase, 'when midnight moans' is, in comparison, feeble. True, the reverberations of the iron tongue of midnight may be felt as moans, yet the alliteration seems mechanical, forcedly calling for a response we are not in this case inclined to give. We are glad the poet has a not impossible she who lightens his darkness, and the 'lattice-gleam' is pretty, but this conclusion does not somehow come off: it is the scene that holds us. Hardy has given us a clue to his intentions in his subtitle, 'Onomatopoeic', which implies that his piece is an exercise in fitting sound to sense. The term may well bring to mind the celebrated

> *Moan of doves in immemorial elms*
> *And murmur of innumerable bees . . .*

and other comfortable sonorities in Tennyson and his Victorian successors, poets who kept their vowels open; but Hardy's effects are quite different. He wants to recreate in his poems whatever interests or moves him, and as we have seen, such interests or emotions are not for him limited by conventions. He is after the truth, and in the world around him he sees nothing common or unclean. He is a Victorian, and he paid melodious and admiring tribute to Tennyson and Swinburne, but in this kind of nature poetry we are reminded of earlier Romantic work—for example, of Coleridge noting the wind moulding the clouds 'in lazy flakes', or the sunset's 'peculiar tint of yellow green'.

The sounds in this poem are sounds of activities, petty goings-on, yet part of the remorseless workings of the elements and of time. Look, to begin with, at the verbs in the first verse: 'creep', 'skims', 'cluck', 'scrabble', 'rot'. There is something sinister about the way the wrinkled ripples form a network over the surface of the stream which is slack only in appearance, and we feel the force and rightness of the odd, pedantic Johnsonian word 'reticulations'. The wind is 'irritable', and we realise that the poet's feelings are inextricably mixed up with what is happening in the scene that meets his gaze. In 'the current clucks' alliteration and rhyming vowels echo the sharp repeated water noises, and the adverb 'smartly' implies quick precise efficiency, and carries overtones of cunning. All hollow places, all weaknesses, are found out and worked on. They are caused by floods, when nature puts forth irresistible powers; but even when the stream is slack, in tiny ways the nagging destruction goes on, and 'years of flood' makes our imaginations reach out in time to feel the endlessness of the whole process. 'Scrabbled' is furtive and bestial and seems to deprive the destructive element of all dignity; the echoing 'hollow place', 'sodden base', makes us hear the repeated petty assaults on the bridge's structure; and the bridge may well stand as a potent symbol of man's efforts at civilisation, his continuing attempts to impose some sort of order on an alien universe.

The last line is an image of beauty's quiet decay. We must notice the hyphen between 'floating' and 'lily,' and read the word as if it were 'water-lily', so that we feel three strong stresses on 'leaves rot fast'. So read, the rhythm thumps the sense into us, and we can see that such an arrangement fits the pattern of the poem, for we have the same heavy triple beat in 'slack stream's face', 'pier's sodden base', 'wistful waiting rows', and 'dark world shows'. The fact that here the stresses end a short line makes a kind of coda, a rhythmic punctuation at the end of the first stanza.

The long lines of the poem have, on the whole, six stresses, the shorter ones four, and the poet disposes of them irregularly according to the fluctuations of the meaning. In the same way he does not tie a standard number of unstressed syllables to the stresses, but varies them too. The whole rhythm follows the vagaries of the moving water, which streams steadily on but within its stream bears eccentric eddies. Half the lines have an odd number of syllables, and I think, though one probably cannot demonstrate the point, that these odd quantities help to give the poem its special flavour.

In the second verse the poet's eye turns from the river to the swallows on the house-top. They too, like the 'gathering swallows'

56

in Keats's *Ode to Autumn* bring in feelings of time and change, for they are 'waiting' to migrate. It is of course the poet who is wistful about all this. Their motion is sudden—they 'arrow off'—and quite unlike the graceful swooping of the birds in the first poem. They drop, and disappear. The river seems to have devoured everything, except for the lady, who stands for light, for guidance, for permanence in the poet's life.

The human figure in *The Sheep Boy* is not the poet but an anonymous lonely boy, peering puzzled witness to nature's goings-on. We hear in the lines Hardy's familiar mixture of duple and triple feet; the form seems to follow the movements of feelings and happenings in the poem, and to be, like the sea-fog that is to blot out the view, both 'flexuous' and 'solid'. We begin with heavy sunshine, and the hollow is a heather-filled purple bowl, like the great trough of a swell in the sea. Hardy shared with Hopkins an intense feeling for what the latter called 'inscape', that uniqueness of form and feeling that is in all the shapes and motions of nature. The curious, rough, ugly word 'entroughed' follows on the sense of 'concave'; 'swell' and 'sway' give us the motion of the sea after a storm; the crests of swells are far apart, so the valley-trough is large. The fact that sea-troughs move and change prepares us for the change from sun to fog, the sense of impermanence even in a solid summer landscape, that the poem dramatises. Two rhymes, which share the same long vowel, tie together the first five lines, whose rhythm, theatrically abrupt at the beginning, widens and extends itself to echo the wave motion of sea and storm, of whose sinister power the wind-fiends are emblems. The country labels, Draäts, and, later, Pokeswell Hills, Kite Hill, give the scene a local habitation and a name. Then comes a quick, staccato, octosyllabic couplet, dry and prosaic, breaking apart the swinging melody of the first sentence. The sudden hum makes a tune, but we can't understand what it is or where it comes from, though our heads turn 'this side, that side', and the verb 'seems' adds to the vagueness. Then we know what is happening. The bees gathering honey in the heather know a change is coming, for nature's creatures are more aware of her workings than puzzled humans are. The line 'With consternation mid their rapt employ' is characteristic of

Hardy's odd diction, and some readers may be put off by what they consider to be its clumsiness. 'Consternation', they might argue, is peculiarly prosaic, and sorts ill with the archaism 'mid' and the literary use of 'employ' for 'employment'. But we might consider that 'consternation' is an apt word for the bees' panic, which causes them in their headstrong flight (they can't navigate in a fog) to bump into the sheep-boy; and that 'rapt' exactly conveys the single-minded concentration of the worker bee.

This section of the poem is concluded by a regular ten-syllable, final-sounding couplet, and the same rhythm begins the next section. The quiet steady regularity of these lines fits the bewilderment of the boy, caught between two apparently unconnected happenings. As the mist appears, the rhythm changes again, following the sinuous movements of the fog, with its contradictory qualities of flexuousness and solidity. The verbs 'sail' and 'travel' add a strong, almost consciously directed sense of powerful movement to the solidity, and lead up to the biblical simile of the pillar of cloud, a climax of power. The sheep-boy fits into the biblical reference, which gives a sense of timelessness to the scene.

The end of the poem contrasts the sun-drenched beauty of the purple hollow and the surrounding hills with the quenched invisibility brought by the fog. Its penultimate lines bring together the boy and the beautiful landscape; 'in a trice' conveys the suddenness of the fog's rising, and the three rhymes help a crescendo of movement, resolved in the long last line, which closes the rhyme left suspended on 'Israelite'. The coined compound 'viewless-folded' is another of Hardy's linguistic fingerprints—the fog makes things invisible, and it envelops them. The vowels in 'folded' and 'scrolls' are close to those of the rhymes of the preceding three lines, and this sameness of sound is a kind of image of the seamless monotony of the fog. 'Creeping scrolls' combines a striking visual image with a feeling of stealth; and the final 'white' (we have already noted its conclusive chime) leaves us with all colour, all form obliterated.

Hardy's verse keeps its freshness and interest because he so successfully adapted traditional rhythms to the needs of his peculiar vision, and developed from them his own tunes. He is original, but not revolutionary. His novels brought him fame, and his house became a shrine for literary pilgrims, but his poetry remains obstinately private and (I do not use the word pejoratively) provincial. That is its strength. It is the clear voice of the thinking and feeling man, echoing the stuff of his daily existence. Selections of his verse are useful to begin with, but any interested reader should get the collected poems, read them, and mark those that strike him. He will find that repeated readings will increase the number of markings, and almost always lead him to poems which he is surprised to have missed before. If he feels daunted by the eight hundred odd pages (we have lost the habit of *reading* verse: we talk about it instead) let him try: '*I look into my glass*'; *Lausanne: In Gibbon's Old Garden*; *A Man*; *The Ruined Maid*; *The Respectable Burgher on the Higher Criticism*; *The Dark-Eyed Gentleman*; *The Abbey Mason*; *In a Waiting Room*; *In St Paul's a While Ago*; '*We are getting to the end*', and *Drinking Song*. If our reader does not find enough variety, energy, sense, feeling, humour, pathos here, he had better stick to prose.

No one who likes Hardy's poems should miss Dr Leavis's brilliant and sympathetic analysis of *After a Journey* in 'Reality and Sincerity', reprinted in *Selections from Scrutiny*, vol. 1. This is the best appraisal of Hardy's greatness that I know.*

Philip Larkin, in a recent *Listener*, said admirably: 'One can read him for years and years and still be surprised. . . . In almost every Hardy poem . . . there is a little spinal cord of thought, and each has a little tune of its own.' Except to add that some of the cords are formidably twisted, and some of the tunes nobly ample, I can think of no better tribute.

* I have tried to place Hardy in relation to his contemporaries in *English Verse: Voice and Movement from Wyatt to Yeats*, Cambridge U.P. 1967.

EDWARD THOMAS
March
Old Man

Commentary by H. Coombes

March

Now I know that Spring will come again,
Perhaps to-morrow: however late I've patience
After this night following on such a day.

While still my temples ached from the cold burning
5   Of hail and wind, and still the primroses
Torn by the hail were covered up in it,
The sun filled earth and heaven with a great light
And a tenderness, almost warmth, where the hail dripped,
As if the mighty sun wept tears of joy.
10 But 'twas too late for warmth. The sunset piled
Mountains on mountains of snow and ice in the west:
Somewhere among their folds the wind was lost,
And yet 'twas cold, and though I knew that Spring
Would come again, I knew it had not come,
15 That it was lost too in those mountains chill.

What did the thrushes know? Rain, snow, sleet, hail,
Had kept them quiet as the primroses.
They had but an hour to sing. On boughs they sang,
On gates, on ground; they sang while they changed perches
20 And while they fought, if they remembered to fight:
So earnest were they to pack into that hour
Their unwilling hoard of song before the moon
Grew brighter than the clouds. Then 'twas no time
For singing merely. So they could keep off silence
25 And night, they cared not what they sang or screamed;
Whether 'twas hoarse or sweet or fierce or soft;
And to me all was sweet: they could do no wrong.

Something they knew—I also, while they sang
And after. Not till night had half its stars
30 And never a cloud, was I aware of silence
Stained with all that hour's songs, a silence
Saying that Spring returns, perhaps to-morrow.

Old Man

Old Man, or Lad's-Love—in the name there's nothing
To one that knows not Lad's-Love, or Old Man,
The hoar-green feathery herb, almost a tree,
Growing with rosemary and lavender.
5   Even to one that knows it well, the names
Half decorate, half perplex, the thing it is:
At least, what that is clings not to the names
In spite of time. And yet I like the names.

The herb itself I like not, but for certain
10   I love it, as some day the child will love it
Who plucks a feather from the door-side bush
Whenever she goes in or out of the house.
Often she waits there, snipping the tips and shrivelling
The shreds at last on to the path, perhaps
15   Thinking, perhaps of nothing, till she sniffs
Her fingers and runs off. The bush is still
But half as tall as she, though it is as old;
So well she clips it. Not a word she says;
And I can only wonder how much hereafter
20   She will remember, with that bitter scent,
Of garden rows, and ancient damson trees
Topping a hedge, a bent path to a door,
A low thick bush beside the door, and me
Forbidding her to pick.

25   As for myself,
Where first I met the bitter scent is lost.
I, too, often shrivel the grey shreds,
Sniff them and think and sniff again and try
Once more to think what it is I am remembering,
30   Always in vain. I cannot like the scent,
Yet I would rather give up others more sweet,
With no meaning, than this bitter one.

I have mislaid the key. I sniff the spray
And think of nothing; I see and I hear nothing;

35   *Yet seem, too, to be listening, lying in wait*
      For what I should, yet never can, remember:
      No garden appears, no path, no hoar-green bush
      Of Lad's-Love, or Old Man, no child beside,
      Neither father nor mother, nor any playmate;
40   *Only an avenue, dark, nameless, without end.*

Increasing urbanisation naturally goes with some degree of dimin-
ution of country life and even of Nature itself, Nature with its
meaning of trees, hedges, flowers, birds, animals and so on; even sea
and sky are more and more invaded, and the earth more and more
built on and its surface more and more rapidly changed. Large
town and city life, not village and market town, are now our norm.

   However, in spite of new towns and spreading rashes of building
everywhere, and of the coming into the world of new hazards of
pollution and destruction (such as the *Torrey Canyon* oil disaster),
and of the growing number of airplanes and of manmade objects
in space, it remains a fact that earth and sea and sky must continue
to be in important senses both our sustenance and our background;
they exist as forces in our living and as available objects for our
delight and contemplation. We can still walk on a wintry spring
day as in the poem *March*; there are still countless gardens in which
parents have encounters with their children, as in *Old Man*.

   It could be said, then, that these poems have a lasting interest; the
world of machines and goods and scientific technology has not
made them irrelevant to our interests. Could we say, in addition,
that they have a universal interest, universal, that is, among readers
of poetry? Would they appeal, for instance, to a reader who had
little interest in Nature as such? We have to remember here that
the phrase 'Nature poetry' suggests a very broad and elastic category.
Just think for a moment of a few well-known poems which would
come into it: Marvell's *Garden*, and Wordsworth's *Tintern Abbey*,
each of them expressing a fusion of delight in immediate environment with profoundly meditative thinking, and yet at the same
time sharply differing from each other, mainly by the presence of a
meaningful wit in Marvell; Hopkins's *Hurrahing in Harvest*, where
rapture in the manifestations of the season and the sky combine
with strong religious feeling to make a kind of Christian-pagan

poem. From the fact that there is so much variety and individuality of approach we can see that we want in our 'Nature' poems to feel something of the poet's particular way of seeing, perceiving, feeling, thinking. With a good poem this sensibility is something we can all, at least to some extent, understand and share. A good Nature poem is in one way or another a good 'human nature' poem.

Can we say 'in a word' what *March* is about? Is it in the main a description of the predominantly physical experiencing of a particular day and evening? Is 'signs of Spring' the subject? Or is the subject 'knowing': possible alternative ways of knowing, the poet's and the thrushes'? We could concentrate on one of these and reasonably argue a case for our choice; but a full reading will show that each is an element in the poem, and that they coalesce—with other things too—to form a unity which is much richer than a first reading might suggest. What we have to ask is, does Edward Thomas show here that his words are powerful enough, delicate enough, to move us to feel that the experience about which he is writing was as meaningful for him as he is tacitly claiming it to have been.

There is no doubt about the keenness with which the physical and sensuous character of the day and evening was felt, or about the skill with which it is rendered. We get a strong feeling of the temples that 'ached from the cold burning/Of hail and wind'; there is no escaping those huge heavy clouds which appear to the poet as 'mountains on mountains of snow and ice in the west'; we are made to accept that the primroses have been really seen and noted, the thrushes watched in their varied movements, and their varied songs and utterances listened to, eagerly and discriminatingly listened to. And after the violent challenging weather and the clamour, we share the silence which comes so beautifully in the last four lines.

I think we are being led to agree, then, that the poet actually did experience, and experience sharply, that particular day. Furthermore there is evidence of a more delicate kind of perceptivity. The apparent paradox 'cold burning' is really an exact and truthful expression. The flood of light is felt as marvellous not only in its vastness but as giving a warm colour to the dripping hail. We feel that the very moment when day passed into evening was noted by the poet as the moment when 'the moon/Grew brighter than the clouds'. He knew too that the birds would know when the time for ending their singing was come. The deepening twilight is indicated by the observation that the sky now had 'half its stars'.

We have to consider to what sort of whole the separate details belong, how they cohere in a meaningful unity. Do they add up to a general feeling about life? Are they, taken together, an expression of disposition, of mood, of character? Do they amount to more than vivid description of externals?

The poem is pervaded by a quality which we may (rather coldly perhaps) call balance. We notice certain juxtapositions: the noise and wind with the silent primroses; the softness of the hour's 'great light' with the 'mountains chill' of the clouds in the west; the clamorous birdsong with the ensuing silence. And from these wholly unobtrusive intimations, and from certain other details, we feel the poet delicately arriving at a conclusion which seems to be saying that not only Spring but happiness will perhaps come tomorrow. We have to be careful, of course, in using large words like 'happiness', but the poem has given us hints that very much more than direct description of natural phenomena is involved: 'As if the mighty sun wept tears of joy' is not simply a pleasant fancy. It reaches out towards desire for a warmth which he knows will be enjoyed when it does come. Then the 'tears of joy', with its intimation of the desired relief, and making us linger on 'joy'— emphasised by the fullstop at the end of the line—is sharply checked by 'But 'twas too late for warmth', and the cold seems almost solid in the western sky. But again there is intense absorption in the birdsong tumult; it fills the consciousness, inducing an almost trancelike state by its varied and utter spontaneity. When finally silence comes, we can hardly tell whether it or the sounds mean most to the poet: both are felt intensely, and we note that 'stained' can mean 'blemished' as well as 'coloured'. A certain wonder of living, conveyed largely in sensuous terms, has followed the day's buffetings; and with the wonder a quiet acceptance of distress as part of life. It is interesting that the thrushes are seen as trying to 'keep off silence/And night'. Is there a hint here that silence, though so strangely beautiful on that evening and though a possible sign of a fine Spring day to follow, is also something that suggests, for the poet, the final silence that engulfs all sound? This question may appear far-fetched, and would probably not occur to a reader unacquainted with Thomas's poetry as a whole. In any case it would seem that even if the suggestion is there it is raised only to be dissolved in the wonder and the hope and the 'to me all was sweet'.

Notice in that sentence, 'And to me all was sweet', how the common adjective, far from having a perfunctory emotional-cliché content, has been selected by the poet from the previous line where it signified a particular quality of sound, and then used to convey his feeling; it helps towards the total impression that sweetness was the residue of the day's battering as of the medley of sounds. Other words may be briefly noted as carrying special weight or significance: the sunset that *piled* the clouds up; that inescapable 'chill' at the end of a line; 'pack' combined with 'hoard', both of them 'unpoetical' in this context but conveying the eagerness the poet wants for the birds pouring out song generously from a hoard which is 'unwilling', unlike a human hoarding. These successes in single words can be matched with other kinds in phrasing and longer sequences. The primroses 'torn by the hail' are connected with his own cold temples, and are given an equal attention, both by the repetition of 'still' and by the tempo and modulation of the voice when reading (either silently or aloud); further, 'temples' and 'torn' are subtly associated with 'tenderness' by alliteration as well as by syntax, suggesting a certain softening in atmosphere and feeling. Then there is the monosyllabic deliberation and assurance of

> *I knew it had not come,*
> *That it was lost too in those mountains chill.*

A similar simplicity with firmness is felt in

> *Not till night had half its stars*
> *And never a cloud.*

The profusion and diversity of bird activity and bustle and song are felt in the clustering together of nouns like boughs, gates, ground, perches, and of the adjectives hoarse, sweet, fierce, soft. And after the noise and movement the concluding quiet seems a very positive thing. This onomatopoeia is functional throughout, helping towards wholeness of impact and impression and not thrusting itself forward for separate attention as a 'beauty'.

I had been acquainted with *March* for quite a long time before I realised how finely it was organised. Incidentally if we use this word in literary criticism—and the same could be said of 'juxta-position' and 'balance'—we have to try to ensure that it does not simply carry the meaning of 'clever arrangement'. The organisation we praise has to have flow. We readily see that the 'perhaps to-morrow' of the opening is repeated at the close, but we may not so quickly notice how Thomas has developed the poem from stage to stage. The first three lines are explicit statement, they give a con-clusion that has been reached at night: 'Now I know . . .' We then go back to the experience which prompted the conclusion, to the day with its storms, its weight of cold, its brief time of 'great light' and a glory when the 'hail dripped'—frozen rain but also melting. Roughly we could say that this section combines the harsh and the kind in Nature: though is 'kind' too unambiguous a word at this juncture? We are also told firmly what he 'knew'. In the next section there is another combination of opposites, that of noise and silence, and we note that it begins with asking what the thrushes 'knew'. The difference between his own mode of knowing and that of the birds, who had also endured the 'rain, snow, sleet, hail', is suggested, and later we have

> *Something they knew—I also, while they sang*
> *And after.*

And finally we are brought round again to the clarity and quiet which promise Spring, 'perhaps to-morrow'.

Perhaps tomorrow, but certainly sometime: 'Spring returns', always returns: but meanwhile there may be much to be endured. This may sound trite and moralistic, but the poem is anything but that; Edward Thomas is not in the least a preacher. He is quietly indicating the tension between patience and hope, but almost all is done by a vivid and sensitive account of his response to natural phenomena. He is as far as may be from analysing himself in abstract terms or offering general comments on life. It is clear that he has 'organised' his material, but the movement of the verse is so natural, so like someone speaking, speaking easily but with precision, and the transitions from part to part are made so inevit-

ably, that we have no sense of laborious or self-conscious arrangement. To put it more positively, the final effect of the way the
rhythm and tempo enforce and combine with the prose-meaning—
steady deliberation, easy flowing, sharp checks, eager outgoing,
quiet returns, easy flow again—is one of finely controlled and yet
spontaneous speech. The tone is quiet and self-assured, the assurance
being of that kind which largely comes of consciousness of strength
in the recording of impressions and what they may mean to a
thoughtful man. Edward Thomas never proclaims his 'findings' in
ringing verse. The delicate honesty is perceived by us, not paraded
by the poet. His poetry is marked by a quiet strength.

The same expression, 'quiet strength', could be used, has in fact
many times been used, for much of Wordsworth's poetry. Moreover there are many Edward Thomas poems which satisfy
Wordsworth's requirement of language really used by men, of
significance in everyday situation and happening. Both *March* and
Old Man do so. They are alike in that, and they share other characteristics too. Yet they are distinct from each other in the way that
two pieces of music by the same composer may be different though
in similar form. The same sensibility, the same hand, are discernible
in both; but we do not speak of repetition. *Old Man* is distinguished from *March* mainly in being more meditative; pondering
is more pervasive in it. Yet 'pondering' seems too restricted and
inexact a word to characterise adequately a poem which integrates
so perfectly a grasp of the present, the actual, with a mental
process which itself combines lucidly stated conjecture—'And I can
only wonder . . .'—with the effort to recall something which the
poet feels to have been and to be profoundly significant for him.
  The substance of the poem is readily enough indicated: an
introduction, with some comment, to the names of the plant; the
little girl and the bush, and the poet wondering what her memories
of it will be in future years; the poet's own smelling of the 'grey
shreds', with more comment; and finally, the fruit of his effort to
recall. Even when we take into account the elusiveness of the nature
of memory, it is astonishing what a subtle and rich poem is made
here out of the simple data. Much has to be taken in before we
reach those uncompromising last four lines. Yet solemn as this

conclusion is, the poem in its wholeness has vitality of sensuous perceiving, precise and vivid unfolding of situation, and powerful rendering of the impression of perplexed seeking in the region of 'the dark backward and abysm of time' (*The Tempest*).

We are left in no doubt as to the nature of the scent of the plant (which, botanically speaking, is southernwood): 'that bitter scent', 'the bitter scent'; he 'cannot like the scent', yet he 'would rather give up others more sweet . . . than this bitter one'. You will have noticed that I omitted three words in that last quotation, and if any phrase may be said to hold the key to this poem, it is perhaps this one: 'with no meaning'. What prompted the poet were the country names of the plant in association with the encounter with his child. Lad's-Love, Old Man: when we have read the poem carefully, do we not feel that in the second line Lad's-Love and Old Man are more facts or essences, youthful love and old age—'the thing it is'— than names? If we have known young love, or know what old age is, shall we not recognise a certain propriety in the names, both love and age carrying a bitterness with them? Nevertheless the plant grows near the sweet-smelling lavender and rosemary. Some readers may feel that there is an echo here of folk-lore and *Hamlet*: 'There's rosemary for you; that's for remembrance'.

The suggestions of youth and age in the names are beautifully enhanced by the man's encounter with the child. And how skilfully this encounter is introduced by the sentence containing his prophecy of what the herb will one day mean to the child:

> . . . *but for certain*
> *I love it, as some day the child . . .*

and we are immediately in her living presence at that particular moment. From our position of vantage we watch her

> . . . *snipping the tips and shrivelling*
> *The shreds at last on to the path,*

and while we are being given the exact picture, we notice also that the poet, casually it seems, slips in a reminder of growth and age:

> *The bush is still*
> *But half as tall as she, though it is as old.*

The father, then, confronts the child, and in the quietest and most unobtrusive manner we are made to feel both how the generations are linked up and how they differ. Both child and father pick from the bush and sniff the scent; she perhaps thinks, 'perhaps of nothing', and he also thinks, though very consciously, and can 'see and hear nothing'; she 'often waits there', he seems to be 'lying in wait'. But there is a radical difference too: after her lingering over the scent, she 'runs off', no doubt blithe and forgetting, forgetting for the moment anyway. The grown man cannot be childishly spontaneous, he must ponder, he must try and try to think what it is he is remembering. In the hint he gives, or more than hint, of what comes into his mind, lies the central poignancy of the poem.

The central poignancy? In the endeavour to take in to the full the feeling and thought of the poem, we might consider some words by Yeats:

> Man is in love and loves what vanishes.
> What more is there to say?

Yeats means that man is in love with life and with the things of the world, and these things are subject to time. This thought is certainly contained in *Old Man*, but it would be a gross simplification to define the feeling of the whole poem as one of grieving over transience. The consciousness out of which Thomas writes, the experience called up by watching the child and by the deep absorption in the scent, are marked as much by endeavour to understand and to state precisely as by any sombre thought or feeling of regret. The final line is of course stark enough:

> Only an avenue, dark, nameless, without end.

The suggestion is undoubtedly of death and eternity, and it is the last line of the poem. But it is hardly the last word, and what we are aware of is not simple bitterness; we still carry in our minds and feelings the peculiar brooding persistency of the poet. It persists as a positive force. Moreover there are many images of activity and quickness to return to: 'plucking' the feathery spray, 'snipping the tips', and running off. And it is no accident that side by side with 'that bitter scent' we are given the line

> Of garden rows, and ancient damson trees.

Have we not suggestions of fertility and sweetness here? Fertility and sweetness in *ancient* trees?

To subtilise and further enhance the mood or condition of mingled bitter-sweet there is the presence of something which is not likely to be noticed by everyone at a first reading: it is something implicit, not stated. This is the co-existence in the poem of emblems or symbols of the known, the inherited, the named, the customary-domestic, with an image of everlasting darkness. The plant has been humanly named, the avenue is nameless; there are the garden's ordered rows, the avenue seems unconfined; the path leads to a door, the avenue is endless. And when he says

Where first I met the bitter scent is lost,

he is not referring only to the actual herb; he is wondering also when he first began to realise that life could be 'bitter'. But despite that realisation, and perhaps all the more intensely because of it, the familiar things of everyday life remain precious to him. The strange quality of the bush itself, the bush whose pretty half-puzzling, half-suggestive names do not express its essential timelessness, exists in his own tended well-loved garden. The child can carelessly and spontaneously run in and out of the house; the grown man is troubled by self-consciousness. Yet it is through this very self-consciousness that his inner life is rich. I do not know whether the key that he has mislaid is the key to a house which he cannot any more live in with happy unself-consciousness, or the key to an understanding of life. Perhaps it is both? It is of course the key to memory also.

Like many of Edward Thomas's poems, *Old Man* is written in a blank verse which though undeniably based on the tones and inflexions of the speaking voice, is never loose and uncontrolled. Ease is not looseness. There is in fact, a union of control and ease which seems perfect for its quietly dramatic purpose: we should emphasise the 'quietly' there. The movement and sound have the variety of tempo and weight and stress, the pauses and changes of direction, which prompt the description 'dramatic'. Little parentheses like 'And yet I like the names' and 'though it is as old' sound conversational but with their reference to names and age are meaningful details in the total structure. Then note how the musing sequence

> *And I can only wonder how much hereafter*
> *She will remember . . .*

is followed by a build-up of phrases giving the details of scene and garden which she may recall in future years; we pause between phrase and phrase, and savour each item, till we are brought up with a slight change of tone on the sharper sound of '. . . and me/Forbidding her to pick'. When he 'shrivels the grey shreds' and sniffs and thinks and sniffs and thinks the rhythm conveys bafflement and persistence; then suddenly the failure, 'always in vain'. In the last four lines, the sounds of the list of negatived living and loved things, culminating pointedly in 'nor any playmate', seem to merge into the solemnity of the final line with something of the effect of daylight objects merging into twilight and darkness.

Edward Thomas's poetry has often been called, and called with approval, 'simple'. Those who have found it so have probably had in mind either his simplicity of diction and syntax or his quiet unassuming tone, perhaps both. Certainly he is among the least pretentious of poets. At the same time he is the reverse of naïve in the way his superb technical finesse subserves the subtle expression of outlook or vision, sensibility, character. The process of self-exploration is integral with a capacity for experiencing certain aspects or areas of life and living with an extraordinary sharpness and depth. Introspection does not inhibit active communion with the phenomenal world, and the issue is poetry which (to use again some words of Yeats) 'bids us touch and taste and hear and see the world'. With *Old Man* in mind we shall want to supply 'and smell'. We shall also want to add that a sense-experience can be the gateway into something truly 'rich and strange'.

The following poems by Thomas may be studied next: *The Sign Post, May the Twenty-third, The Other, Wind and Mist, Haymaking, As the Team's Head-Brass, And You Helen, A Gentleman.*

JON SILKIN
Worm
Violet

Commentary by Terry Eagleton

Worm

Look out, they say, for yourself.
The worm doesn't. It is blind
As a sloe; its death by cutting,
Bitter. Its oozed length is ringed,
5   With parts swollen. Cold and blind
It is graspable, and writhes
In your hot hand; a small snake, unvenomous.
Its seeds furred and moist
It sexes by lying beside another,
10   In its eeking conjunction of seed
Wriggling and worm-like.
Its ganglia are in its head,
And if this is severed
It must grow backwards.
15   It is lowly, useful, pink. It breaks
Tons of soil, gorging the humus
Its whole length; its shit a fine cast
Coiled in heaps, a burial mound, or like a shell
Made by a dead snail.
20   It has a life, which is virtuous
As a farmer's, making his own food.
Passionless as a hoe, sometimes, persistent.
Does not want to kill a thing.

Violet

The lobed petals receive
Each other's nestling shape.

We share the sun's beneficence:
Frost, men, snowdrops.
5   Then the violet unfolds. Not an uncasing
Of the corolla, each petal compliant
To the purpose of survival, obedient to that; but as it feels
The sun's heat, that puberty
Pushes out from its earlier self-clasping

76

10   *Two distinct, clenched halves. Stiffens then.*
      These fluttering portions that made
      The bud, separately elect
      To be the flower; the violet
      Halves itself, pushing apart
15   *In two separate forces;*
      It divides up itself, it becomes two violet portions.
      It is not a conformation of members,
      Each petal a tooth, an eyelash.
      On the other hand, the violet is torn apart.
20   *Its increase is by dividing;*
      Its stiffened petals push further apart.
      It adheres to its nature; it has no maturity,
      Other than this.
      It requires courage, and finds that
25   *In this unclasping of its self-worship: two palms tentatively*
      Open. Going both ways,
      They absorb a huge circle
      Of violeted air, an intent
      Movement of embrace;
30   *Created, exposed, powerful.*
      The air is coloured somewhat violet.
      It costs itself much.

There is a sense in which the 'meaning' of *Worm* lies as much in the whole conception of writing with this intent seriousness about a worm as in the detail of what is actually said. The reader is confronted from the title onwards, implicitly and rather casually, with a general issue—the issue of what kind of subject matter is appropriate to poetry—and the way in which the poem does not explicitly confront its own unorthodoxy, in dealing with such concentration with what might be held as slight material, seems itself a distinctive stance on the poet's part. His refusal to justify his subject matter suggests from the outset a kind of moral challenge to the reader, the more successful in its casual undermining of conventional expectations for being implicit rather than didactic. The very way the poem presents itself to the reader suggests already a certain range of moral values, perspectives and decisions, manifested in its title, content and approach; in what it does not say, or argue out, as much as in what it does. One could imagine a comic or symbolic or bathetic poem about a worm, but this poem's very refusal to use these techniques seems to suggest that there is something of serious value to be gained in merely observing a worm closely, in its integral mode of being.

The poem offers a curious ambiguity. On the one hand it refuses to elaborate profound meanings from the worm, presenting itself as a self-consciously minor, competent job aware of its own limits, an undramatic series of precise and dispassionate jottings. On the other hand, in tension with this grim, economical empiricism, is a sense that the poet *is* somehow getting at more than is empirically there, that there is a subterranean working of a deeper significance slightly in excess of the observed facts, which is allowed momentarily to emerge, or to come through as a resonance beneath the descriptive neutrality. The very slightness of the poem seems to be charged with a kind of significance; it does not foist symbolic meanings directly onto the worm (in fact most of the time it is concerned with refusing such an approach), but it does, even so, suggest by a latently dramatic tension of tone and syntax, and by its unwavering, myopic seriousness of focused attention, a sense that there is something of moral value to be grasped here, something almost defiantly in excess of what a worm's life would seem to lend itself to. Whether this excess is fanciful or creative is a central criterion for deciding the poem's success. In any case, the reader is confused: if he feels that too much is being made, morally, of the worm, he is prevented from formulating this into a critical assault because the poem itself seems also at another level to confirm this response, rigorously limiting moral elaboration.

I think that it is around this ambiguity that the poem's central meanings crystallise. The technical tension within the poem, between simply observing the worm precisely and allowing a deeper kind of statement to emerge, is also a moral tension: a preoccupation with recording non-human life-forms in their intrinsic alienness from man, and simultaneously feeling after their human relevance. The poem does not simply treat the worm as something symbolic or emblematic of human life; it aims at some kind of intermediate dimension where non-human life can be grasped both in its own, self-contained modes and simultaneously in its oblique relation to human existence.

This tension is developed at one level in the way the poem blends a neutrally descriptive tone and syntax with a quietly dramatic sense of moral meaning. The first line—'Look out, they say, for yourself'—is casually colloquial, but lent a certain dramatic poise and weight by the careful (too careful?) placing of 'they say'. The next short sentence—'The worm doesn't'—is again casual statement, yet also curtly dramatic. 'It is blind/As a sloe' links the worm, in 'blind', to a human quality, but then preserves a sense of the worm's alienness by making a comparison, not with human life, but with another animal. Similarly, 'its death by cutting, /Bitter' endows the worm with a certain rhetorical dignity (although is 'bitter' descriptive of the worm's experience or of a human reading of it?), but the next phrase—'its oozed length is ringed . . .'—counterpoises this dignity by getting, with admirable economy, a felt sense of the worm's strangeness (one feels the word 'bitter' carry over here into our reactions to this pungent description). The worm is 'Cold and blind', but also 'graspable': the shift there from line 5 to line 6 is also a sudden shift in moral perspective, a movement from the worm seen in itself to the worm as related to man. Now there is a slight, complex tension between worm and man: the worm can be grasped, and moves, yet its movement is an inhuman snakelike writhing; on the other hand it writhes in the human hand, its cold life contiguous to hot human life, and it is, after all, only a small, unvenomous snake, which is both observed description and a way of making the worm more morally sympathetic to man, modifying its distastefulness. The next lines describe the worm objectively, almost scientifically (and notice how the consciously naïve adjective 'worm-like' hints at the limits of human, interpretative language, the inability to describe the worm as anything but itself); the reference to the cutting of the head suggests, poignantly, the worm's vulnerable, inhuman passivity. Yet the next lines again counterpoise this, allowing the worm's human significance to emerge more fully: it is 'lowly, useful, pink'. Notice the technique there: the first two adjectives are moral and relate the worm to man, building up to a slight climax where one expects another, evaluative term. Instead we get the conscious anticlimax of 'pink', a straight factual term:

once again the poem just holds back from the edge of moral interpretation.

The sentence—'It breaks/Tons of soil . . .'—is significant: it is a kind of justification at the *factual* level of the *moral* centrality which the poem gives to the worm, by stressing that, in practical terms, the worm *has* a function disproportionate to its seeming capacity. Its breaking of the soil seems to have a human purposiveness about it, yet 'gorging' again hints at the inhuman alienness; the worm is humanly purposive, yet in an unconscious, automatic, machine-like way.

In the next movement of the poem we get a brief, complex interrelation of organic and inorganic life which seems a small symbol of the poem's general theme. The worm (organic life) has excrement (inorganic) like the shell (inorganic) of a dead snail (both inorganic and organic). In the final lines, the full moral meaning of the worm is allowed to come to the surface. It is a humble, functional, non-competitive, non-dominative form of life, like a virtuous farmer, and this is admired; yet the response is complex, because we are made to feel simultaneously how these virtues derive from its alienness: its blind, inhumanly 'persistent', self-enclosed activity, its lack of relations with other lives, its incapacity for feeling ('passionless'), its narrow, insensitive and yet at the same time humble and useful persistence in its own form of being. It shares the human qualities of a farmer, but also the blunt objectivity of a hoe.

What is remarkable about this poem is the exact matching of form and content, of what is said and how it is said. The 'otherness' of the worm is enacted in the dispassionate, observing precision of the style (notice how metaphor is avoided and weight thrown upon the exactly delineating quality of individual adjectives); but this very dispassionateness is a kind of strength. Steady observation, the poem implies, is itself a moral good, as indeed it is in the case of the worm. The final line—'Does not want to kill a thing' clinches the whole movement: it is a direct moral (one might say, political) statement, but the omission of the pronoun prevents this from sounding over-rhetorical and gives it an air of casual description.

The second Silkin poem I want to discuss, *Violet*, is perhaps best seen as a more ambitious attempt in the same genre. This, again, seems to be a poem aiming at some intermediate dimension between natural and human life. An actual violet is taken, the inward workings of its life recorded in intense, closely sensuous detail (notice how different this fidelity to detail is from conventional 'Nature' poetry), and yet simultaneously a human resonance, a sense of how this autonomous, self-enclosed life relates to human knowledge, is allowed to emerge, sustaining but rarely dominating the observation of the flower. As in the first poem, the poet achieves this 'double-focusing' by a number of techniques. Notice, for instance, the way in which this is done through careful variations in rhythm and syntax, alternating long, slightly rhetorical and dramatic generalisations with short, elliptical, descriptive sentences. Notice also how this double-effect, of simultaneously observing and reflecting morally on the flower, is achieved by a blending of rather abstract, latinate diction with concrete, sensuous verbs and adjectives. The total effect of this blending, as with *Worm*, is to produce an ambiguity: the poem presents itself as a controlled, steady record of observed detail, but it also goes beyond this into metaphor and generalised reflection. The poet clearly could not have elicited all this detail from simply looking hard at the violet, since what he describes is a process in time; but the achievement of the poem is to give this deeper exploration, and the moral meanings which go with it, the appearance of realistic description.

The first two lines seem a conventional enough opening, although there is a hint here of an idea which will be developed later: the petals are individuated, each given an unfolding life of its own, and so able to 'receive' each other, as if by conscious choice. Each petal both receives and nestles, and each of these verbs contains both an active and a passive element; so the effect of these introductory lines is to suggest both the passive, interlocking unity of the flower, and the autonomous activity of each of its parts. Next there is a swift change of perspective to moral generalisation (note the abstract, rhythmical poise of 'beneficence'), but the riding balance of this phrase is not allowed to get out of hand. The three curt, concrete nouns which follow ('Frost, men, snowdrops') anchor us back into specificity by a deft change of rhythm. In the casual placing of 'men' in that line, the problem of the relation between men and Nature is sounded for the first time.

The violet's unfolding is then described, but in a way which disturbs conventional expectations. The unfolding is not an integrated, organic process ('each petal compliant . . . obedient to that'— notice again here the use of abstract, latinate diction); it is seen as a forceful, disjointed, almost violent action, as the shift to explosive consonants, hard assonance and stabbing emphasis in 'that puberty . . . Stiffens then' makes clear. This refusal to see the flower as a harmonious whole is underlined by the fact that the motivating power of its unfolding shifts three times; first it is, abstractly, the flower's 'puberty', then the separate decision of the buds, and only then the violet itself. With 'these fluttering portions . . .' we return to an abstract, rhetorical mode of statement, although note how the careful balance of sound in the phrase 'separately elect' is both morally generalised, and yet suggestive of a force of deliberate, gathering decision. This is followed by the build-up of slight dramatic crisis, as the flower halves itself. Notice the way repetition ('the violet/Halves itself . . ./It divides up itself, it becomes two violet portions') gets a slightly breathless, naïve sense of climax which contrasts with the rhetorical equilibrium which has gone before. The same contrast is worked in the next three lines: again we get a rather circumlocutory description, as in lines 5–7, of what the violet is not ('It is not a conformation of members . . .'), and again this refusal of abstract harmony is enacted by a shift to sudden, concrete action:

On the other hand, the violet is torn apart.

The next two lines provide a useful instance of the way the poem integrates moral comment and concrete description into the same tone: 'Its increase is by dividing' is a general reflection, but made to sound, by its closeness to the straight observation of 'Its stiffened petals push further apart', like a statement of the same order.

The final movement of the poem brings out the moral significance of the flower more clearly. We are reminded first, as a kind of warning against fanciful interpretations, that the violet 'adheres to its nature': it has a maturity, even a 'courage', and its struggling expenditure of energy is admired, but these qualities find expression simply *in* the act of its unfolding—the unfolding and maturity have no meaning beyond themselves. The flower's activity is circular, both literally, as it absorbs a 'huge circle of violeted (with a hint of *violated*?) air', and metaphorically, in that its unfolding and self-dividing are done simply for their own sakes, with no meaning or value beyond this. So we are left, as at the end of *Worm*, with a complex, ambivalent response. The violet has a powerful courage, a kind of radical abandonment of self seen in its capacity to emerge from inbound unity into total, disjointed self-exposure; yet like the worm it is merely, in displaying these virtues, adhering to its nature, in a narrow, blind and circular process. Again, as with the worm, we respond to the violet's purposive activity, and thus to what we know of human puberty and self-discovery, at the same time as we are acutely aware of its passive, exposed vulnerability, its inability to be anything other than what it is. The passive vulnerability of both worm and violet connect them to the human at the same time as they distance them from it: there is something morally admirable, yet also alien and slightly fanatical, in this wholly committed, relentless abandonment of self. Two points in *Violet* reinforce this latter sense: first (an idea touched on above), the fact that the violet's lavish self-expenditure is, humanly viewed, purposeless, an outgoing of energy made only for the sake of self-achievement; second, that the violet's maturity, unlike man's, rests not in self-integration but in what is almost self-destruction. One can feel the human undertones in this—the suggestion that man, too, must abandon false integrity for a dangerous yet creative self-exposure—while feeling, simultaneously, the points of difference between man and flower.

Perhaps it is possible to attempt some evaluation of the poem as a whole by asking how far the poet himself seems aware of these points of difference between man and flower. My own feeling is that in this poem Silkin just fails to achieve that sense of simultaneous similarity-and-difference between man and Nature which he got in *Worm*, and that this failure comes from an over-readiness to sympathise with the flower, to read human meanings into it, to—one might almost say—sentimentalise it. On the whole this tendency is held in check, and is not permitted to spoil the poem's achievement; but whereas in *Worm* the creature dealt with could be seen both as a moral corrective to disruptive human tendencies *and* as a life-form strange to man, the attention focused by *Violet* on the inward struggles and impulses of the flower seems to imbue it with a meaning in excess of the realist observation. This is partly a consequence of the difficulty of the subject matter, of choosing a violet in the first place; whereas a worm has a naturally active existence which, as the image of the farmer implies, connects at a simple factual level with human creation, the violet has no such obvious or active relation to human life. In a sense, it is this latter assumption which *Violet* sets out to question: the poem's emphasis on the flower's inwardly active being is meant to challenge the facile view that flowers are merely passive and organic wholes, animated by none of the conflict of impulses which characterises man. In breaking through this false mode of perception, the poem succeeds in establishing an original and creative insight; yet the price of this is, perhaps inevitably, an endowing of the flower with a rhetorical dignity and purposive consciousness which the insistence on its inhuman adherence to its own nature cannot quite modify. Again, this comes through as a quality of tone and style: one feels here, as one did not feel in *Worm*, that even the curt, neutrally recording sentences have a certain pontificating artificiality about them which slightly belies their supposed function within the poem. In my own view, *Violet* is still a successful poem; its defects can best be seen as the price which the poem has to pay for pushing the mode of exploration attempted in *Worm* to a deeper, more ambitious level of statement, and so raising problems of style and approach which cannot, within this poem at least, be fully resolved.

NOTE. *Worm* has so far appeared only in the periodical, *Stand* (vol. 8 no. 1), while *Violet* is part of the collection, *Nature with Man*, to which readers are referred for other poems by Silkin upon the theme expressed in the title.

D. H. LAWRENCE
Snake
Last Lesson of the Afternoon

Commentary by Anthony Beal

Snake

A snake came to my water-trough
On a hot, hot day, and I in pyjamas for the heat,
To drink there.

In the deep, strange-scented shade of the great dark carob-tree
5 I came down the steps with my pitcher
And must wait, must stand and wait, for there he was at the
      trough before me.

He reached down from a fissure in the earth-wall in the gloom
And trailed his yellow-brown slackness soft-bellied down,
      over the edge of the stone trough
And rested his throat upon the stone bottom,
10 And where the water had dripped from the tap, in a small
      clearness,
He sipped with his straight mouth,
Softly drank through his straight gums, into his slack long
      body,
Silently.

Someone was before me at my water-trough,
15 And I, like a second comer, waiting.

He lifted his head from his drinking, as cattle do,
And looked at me vaguely, as drinking cattle do,
And flickered his two-forked tongue from his lips, and mused
      a moment,
And stooped and drank a little more,
20 Being earth-brown, earth-golden from the burning bowels of
      the earth
On the day of Sicilian July, with Etna smoking.

The voice of my education said to me
He must be killed,
For in Sicily the black, black snakes are innocent, the gold are
      venomous.

25   And voices in me said, If you were a man
      You would take a stick and break him now, and finish him
          off.

      But must I confess how I liked him,
      How glad I was he had come like a guest in quiet, to drink at
          my water-trough
      And depart peaceful, pacified, and thankless,
30   Into the burning bowels of this earth?

      Was it cowardice, that I dared not kill him?
      Was it perversity, that I longed to talk to him?
      Was it humility, to feel so honoured?
      I felt so honoured.

35   And yet those voices:
      If you were not afraid, you would kill him!

      And truly I was afraid, I was most afraid,
      But even so, honoured still more
      That he should seek my hospitality
40   From out the dark door of the secret earth.

      He drank enough
      And lifted his head, dreamily, as one who has drunken,
      And flickered his tongue like a forked night on the air, so black
      Seeming to lick his lips,
45   And looked around like a god, unseeing, into the air,
      And slowly turned his head,
      And slowly, very slowly, as if thrice adream,
      Proceeded to draw his slow length curving round
      And climb again the broken bank of my wall-face.
50   And as he put his head into that dreadful hole,
      And as he slowly drew up, snake-easing his shoulders, and
          entered farther,
      A sort of horror, a sort of protest against his withdrawing into
          that horrid black hole,

Deliberately going into the blackness, and slowly drawing
    himself after,
Overcame me now his back was turned.

55   I looked round, I put down my pitcher,
I picked up a clumsy log
And threw it at the water-trough with a clatter.

I think it did not hit him,
But suddenly that part of him that was left behind convulsed
    in undignified haste,
60   Writhed like lightning, and was gone
Into the black hole, the earth-lipped fissure in the wall-front,
At which, in the intense still noon, I stared with fascination.

And immediately I regretted it.
I thought how paltry, how vulgar, what a mean act!
65   I despised myself and the voices of my accursed human
    education.

And I thought of the albatross,
And I wished he would come back, my snake.

For he seemed to me again like a king,
Like a king in exile, uncrowned in the underworld,
70   Now due to be crowned again.

And so, I missed my chance with one of the lords
Of life.
And I have something to expiate;
A pettiness.

Last Lesson of the Afternoon

When will the bell ring, and end this weariness?
How long have they tugged the leash, and strained apart,
My pack of unruly hounds! I cannot start
Them again on a quarry of knowledge they hate to hunt,
5   I can haul them and urge them no more.

No longer now can I endure the brunt
Of the books that lie out on the desks; a full threescore
Of several insults of blotted pages, and scrawl
Of slovenly work that they have offered me.
10 I am sick, and what on earth is the good of it all?
What good to them or me, I cannot see!

                        So, shall I take
My last dear fuel of life to heap on my soul
And kindle my will to a flame that shall consume
15 Their dross of indifference; and take the toll
Of their insults in punishment?—I will not!—

I will not waste my soul and my strength for this.
What do I care for all that they do amiss!
What is the point of this teaching of mine, and of this
20 Learning of theirs? It all goes down the same abyss.

What does it matter to me, if they can write
A description of a dog, or if they can't?
What is the point? To us both, it is all my aunt!
And yet I'm supposed to care, with all my might.

25 I do not, and will not; they won't and they don't; and that's
    all!
I shall keep my strength for myself; they can keep theirs as
    well.
Why should we beat our heads against the wall
Of each other? I shall sit and wait for the bell.

The first sentence of each of these poems makes an immediate
dramatic impact. Both are simple direct statements which involve
us with the 'I' of the poems, engage our interest and arouse expect-
ancy as to what is to follow. The effectiveness of any statement
depends on the writer's choice and arrangement of words and we
should start by taking a closer look at these, using *Snake* as the
example.

After reading the first three stanzas (lines 1–13) a few times, one
striking fact emerges: nearly every word is a monosyllable. These

common, simple words hit us with their immediacy—'a hot, hot day', 'must wait, must stand and wait'. And when the one word in ten which is longer comes, it gains additional strength in this context, standing out as it would not do if surrounded by more complex words.

The first one 'water' is usual enough, but here carries just that extra stress to make us pause to consider it as something more than an everyday thing, rather as something, that both man and snake need for life. 'Pyjamas' is an unexpected word, and an exotic one particularly in this noonday setting. It helps to set the scene, but also something of the character of the man. This is to be the only description of his appearance throughout the poem: 'I in pyjamas'— a suggestion of informality, of being at ease and in tune with his natural surroundings. And how cunningly it is placed in the middle of the simple words and with 'I' in the trebly emphasised heat:

On a hot, hot day, and I in pyjamas for the heat.

In line 4 the exotic setting is again emphasised by 'scented' and 'carob', and in line 8 two-syllable words come three at a time:

And trailed his yellow-brown slackness soft-bellied down,

These words have the effect of slowing down the movement of the verse to the movement of the snake. They seem to make a fairly conventional twelve-syllable line of English verse—but, of course, they are not the complete line. It goes on—

over the edge of the stone trough

and as these short simple words fall over the edge of the line, as it were, after the slowly measured movement that preceded them, we immediately feel and see the snake give its sickening lurch forward.

These are the briefest of comments on the vocabulary and movement of the early lines and need to be expanded and continued throughout the poem to see the full effects. The structure of the complete poem also needs to be examined. We soon note for example

that each separate stanza is one complete sentence and vice versa—
with one exception (where and why?). But in a poem (as in a
symphony) there is nearly always a number of things going on at the
same time. All are interconnected and contribute to the total effect,
but it is impossible to analyse them all simultaneously, so we must
now go on to investigate some other strands in the total fabric of the
poem.

The first two sentences set the scene, introduce the two characters
and indicate the situation: the snake's primacy at the well. All this is
done in a very simple direct way. There is no unnecessary detail to
detract from the clear presentation of the situation. But as the poem
progresses the original themes are both repeated and more sharply
defined. Thus 'heat' becomes 'Sicilian July' and 'the intense still
noon'; the snake who first merely drinks 'as cattle do' becomes 'a
guest', 'honoured', 'like a god', 'a king', 'one of the lords of life'.
The transformation of the plain snake of the first line to a lord of
life at the end is paralleled by the degradation of the man who is at
first ready to treat the snake as a guest, but commits an act which he
later regards as 'paltry', 'vulgar', 'mean' and 'petty'.

The setting of the poem recalls a biblical encounter: a confrontation at a well in the noonday heat of a Mediterranean summer
where one of the participants is apparently endowed with godlike
characteristics. The man is happy to behave as a hospitable host and
let the snake drink first, but these generous impulses are counter-
manded by 'the voice of my education', 'voices in me', 'those
voices', 'the voices of my accursed human education'. Never 'my
voice'.

This is the heart of the poem. One might well argue with
Lawrence's terms. He seems to be saying that if he were an un-
educated man he would not have thrown the log at the snake. But
how would a primitive man—how would an animal for that matter
—react to the sight of a snake? With fear and a desire to get rid of
it? Is hospitality itself a product of human education or an instinctive
feeling?

'Education' incites him to violence. But the deed done, the poet
reacts against it. In the ninth stanza (lines 31-4) there is a series of
staccato shots of self-accusation, ending with an affirmation of
humility. Human education says kill him: not to cowardice. Yet

his natural feeling—to talk to the snake—is this perverse? To feel honoured by its presence—is this humility? The throwing of the log makes both man and snake undignified: an act of aggression is a mean act.

The poet is looking back to a world before the Fall, when man and animals lived together in harmony and mutual self-respect. Man should admire the snakiness of the snake, and the snake respect the manliness of man. It is ironical that in mythology it was the serpent itself that brought about the end of this golden age. But Lawrence does not see the snake as the Old Testament symbol of evil, but rather as one of the dark subterranean gods coming out of 'the burning bowels of the earth' and returning again into the blackness, uncrowned king of the underworld. Indeed the fascination that it holds for Lawrence springs from its independence from man. 'Human education' has enabled man to tame or shame most creatures. He has sentimentalised bears and taught tigers to do tricks and yoked elephants to be beasts of burden. Only the snake has retained its integrity and its separateness, and for this reason Lawrence longs to 'talk' to it—to take a chance with one of the lords of life, to explore a mode of existence so foreign to his human one. But he is prevented by the limitations of his humanity, the indoctrination which century by century has said to men: 'Snakes are dangerous: kill them'.

By referring to the albatross (line 66), Lawrence deliberately draws a parallel between his poem and Coleridge's *Ancient Mariner*. Here the mariner, prompted again by the voices of education, shoots the bird which has been a welcome guest. After the suffering and repentance he undergoes for his callousness, he begins to see in God's creatures 'their beauty and their happiness.' Specifically it is the water-snakes (and this may have jerked the string of recollection in Lawrence's mind) that bring about the mariner's conversion:

> O *happy living things! no tongue*
> *Their beauty might declare:*
> *A spring of love gushed from my heart,*
> *And I blessed them unaware:*

It is a parallel situation and it would be an interesting exercise to compare the two poems further. Basically Coleridge's, or the mariner's, final attitude is one of all-embracing love for God's creatures. Lawrence's is not that, but rather a desire to share in unknown modes of being and escape from the conformist 'educated' limitations of ordinary daily life. Both poems make the reader question his own feelings and his own morality towards the whole animal kingdom.

These themes of education and conformity are obviously also dominant in *Last Lesson of the Afternoon*, but before exploring these further, it is worth noting some obvious differences between the two poems. Merely by looking at the appearance of the poems on the page, or by reading the first lines of each, it is apparent that *Last Lesson* is the more conventional. It has rhymes, the lines are all much the same length. *Snake* is in free verse: indeed it is impossible to conceive of its being written in any other form. How could the effects of the poem have been achieved within a more regular framework? As Lawrence himself wrote in his preface to *New Poems*: 'Free verse has its own *nature* . . . neither star nor pearl, but instantaneous like plasm. . . . It has no finish. It has no satisfying stability, satisfying that is for those who like the immutable. None of this. It is the instant, the quick; the very jetting source of all will-be and has-been.'

Though written in general terms, this might stand as a perfect description of the way free verse works in *Snake*.

Last Lesson is *more* conventional, though still by no means in a rigid framework. Both the lines and the rhyme schemes are irregular, but does their irregularity in any way help what is going on in the poem? Do the rhymes themselves help or hinder? This is a more static poem than *Snake* and does not need the same variations of movement in the verse to match the physical actions and the changing feelings that it describes. *Last Lesson* is much more on one note throughout.

The first line makes an immediate impression with its eight simple monosyllables leading up to the heavy weight of 'weariness'. It is a line which will find an echo in the heart of anyone who has ever been to school, though not everybody will have realised that teachers can long as ardently for the end of lessons as their pupils do. One has to remember that Lawrence was teaching sixty years ago under a much more authoritarian system than exists today. As the poem makes clear, he is supposed to be teaching a class of sixty children, a situation which makes nonsense of the word 'education'. To keep such a number in order is a problem by itself, while to get them all interested in learning is an almost impossible task.

The first two stanzas state the situation and reveal the writer's despair. The third stanza makes the turning point in the poem. The short broken first line strikes the note of crisis: shall he summon up his last energies to revenge himself on his pupils for their insulting response to his teaching? There is no hesitation in the answer, which ends the stanza; and the remainder of the poem hammers home the point that it is not worth wasting soul and strength on this pointless teaching.

The crisis is remarkably similar to that in *Snake*: to give way to violence or not? It is rejected in *Last Lesson* because both the teacher and his pupils are seen as the rather pathetic victims of a bad system. What a negation it is of what human life and true education should be. There is no real personal communication between them. There is nothing to feel deeply about. Nobody cares, and where there is apathy there is no violence.

But in *Snake* the confrontation between man and animal is a highly charged one, always potentially explosive. Lawrence is so struck by the power and beauty of the snake that his reaction must be passionate. That it is one of momentary violent rejection he would trace back to the classroom scene where both teaching and learning are mechanical. What is the point of writing 'a description of a dog'? Men should apprehend other creatures as vivid living beings. The education he is protesting about inculcates mechanical rules, conformity, a fear of the unusual, and a policy of safety first (kill snakes!). It is the enemy of rich natural life.

Snake is undoubtedly the more powerful of these two poems— more powerful in its theme, more subtle and complex in its feeling and action. Moreover, the form of the poem seems perfect, by which I mean that one cannot see how this experience could have been satisfactorily conveyed in any other way—in prose or in rhymed verse or in conventional blank verse. *Last Lesson* is a striking and unusual poem, but there is not the same sense of splendid inevitability about it. Perhaps the poet does protest a little too much. Might not the poem have worked just as well with a different verse pattern, a more regular rhyme scheme? Indeed, might not he have made his point even more effectively in a passage of prose or dramatic dialogue?

When Lawrence wrote *Last Lesson* he was an unknown young man teaching in a South London school. He wrote *Snake* while staying at Taormina in Sicily in July 1920, when he was some ten years older and already recognised as an outstanding writer. There is ten year's more experience behind *Snake*, but this does not altogether explain the difference of quality between the two poems. Lawrence was above all a novelist concerned with human relationships: these he portrayed in much greater depth in his fiction than in his verse. Against *Last Lesson* one should set some of the passages about school in his novel, *The Rainbow*.

What distinguishes Lawrence as a poet is the immediacy of his perceptions, 'the instant, the quick' as he said of free verse. Human relations cannot be immediately apprehended in all their richness and complexity. But the world of nature can be so perceived. And Lawrence's poetry is at its finest when he is writing about animals, birds and flowers. The instinctive awareness of the 'feel', the way of life of an animal, so well demonstrated in *Snake*, is to be found again in *Kangaroo*, *Bat*, *The Mosquito*, *Humming Bird* and others. These are all in free verse, each with its individual cadences and rhythms and and repetitions, its own particular speed and movement appropriate to the subject. And always Lawrence sees these creatures as having their own right to a legitimate place in the world independent of man. They are not idealised like the skylarks and nightingales of the Romantics, or symbols, like the tiger and lambs of Blake.

Although these animal poems show Lawrence at his best, there is much more that is rewarding in his verse. The same imaginative sympathy he shows for beasts and birds also appears in his poems about childhood: *Discord in Childhood* and *Baby Running Barefoot* are two of the finest. His successful poems about adults are always those where he catches a fleeting emotion—such as *After the Opera*, *Sorrow* or *Piano*—rather than those where he tries to explore a more complicated relationship.

Towards the end of his life he wrote a group of poems in a new style—*Bavarian Gentians*, *The Argonauts* and *The Ship of Death*.

These are still in free verse, but in a graver and more formal style drawing on mythology and reading at times like incantations. They are the poems of a dying man, lacking some of the quickness and vividness of the earlier animal poems but displaying a new aspect of his genius not found elsewhere in his verse or prose.

TED HUGHES
Hawk Roosting
An Otter

Commentary by Allan Grant

Hawk Roosting

I sit in the top of the wood, my eyes closed.
Inaction, no falsifying dream
Between my hooked head and hooked feet:
Or in sleep rehearse perfect kills and eat.

5   The convenience of the high trees!
The air's buoyancy and the sun's ray
Are of advantage to me;
And the earth's face upward for my inspection.

My feet are locked upon the rough bark.
10   It took the whole of Creation
To produce my foot, my each feather:
Now I hold Creation in my foot

Or fly up, and revolve it all slowly—
I kill where I please because it is all mine.
15   There is no sophistry in my body:
My manners are tearing off heads—

The allotment of death.
For the one path of my flight is direct
Through the bones of the living.
20   No arguments assert my right:

The sun is behind me.
Nothing has changed since I began.
My eye has permitted no change.
I am going to keep things like this.

An Otter

I

Underwater eyes, an eel's
Oil of water body, neither fish nor beast is the otter:
Four-legged yet water-gifted, to outfish fish;
With webbed feet and long ruddering tail
5   And a round head like an old tomcat.

Brings the legend of himself
From before wars or burials, in spite of hounds and vermin-
poles;
Does not take root like the badger. Wanders, cries;
Gallops along land he no longer belongs to;
10   Re-enters the water by melting.

Of neither water nor land. Seeking
Some world lost when first he dived, that he cannot come at
since,
Takes his changed body into the holes of lakes;
As if blind, cleaves the stream's push till he licks
15   The pebbles of the source; from sea

To sea crosses in three nights
Like a king in hiding. Crying to the old shape of the starlit
land,
Over sunken farms where the bats go round,
Without answer. Till light and birdsong come
20   Walloping up roads with the milk wagon.

II

The hunt's lost him. Pads on mud,
Among sedges, nostrils a surface bead,
The otter remains, hours. The air,
Circling the globe, tainted and necessary,

25   Mingling tobacco-smoke, hounds and parsley,
Comes carefully to the sunk lungs.
So the self under the eye lies,
Attendant and withdrawn. The otter belongs

30   In double robbery and concealment—
From water that nourishes and drowns, and from land
That gave him his length and the mouth of the hound.
He keeps fat in the limpid integument

7   *Reflections live on. The heart beats thick,*
    Big trout muscle out of the dead cold;
35 *Blood is the belly of logic; he will lick*
    The fishbone bare. And can take stolen hold

    On a bitch otter in a field full
    Of nervous horses, but linger nowhere.
    Yanked above hounds, reverts to nothing at all,
40 *To this long pelt over the back of a chair.*

A poet does not write the same poem twice. Putting side by side
two poems by the same author makes us see them as more than
variations on a theme. Although he has written on other subjects,
Ted Hughes is probably best known for his poems about animals,
poems which celebrate natural and animal energies. Yet this does
not tell us much about individual poems. Hawk and otter are not
interchangeable symbols; not only are they different in essential
qualities, they inhabit different worlds. Compare, for example, the
hawk's relation to the sun and the air with the otter's to earth, air
and water. To the hawk the authority and advantage (in this respect
like the fighter pilot of the Second World War) it gains from the
sun is single and immediate; the sun is 'behind' it in both senses. To
the otter, on the other hand, the air is both 'tainted' and 'necessary'.
The world of the hawk is timeless and the hawk itself is a permanent
feature of existence whereas the otter lives through memory and in a
process, stoically engaged in retracing an irrevocable history. We
note other differences in their relation to the world of human
values. There is a black humour to be found in the hawk's egotistical
stance, but we admire the impossible stoicism of the otter, and we
lament, without sentimentalising, its death. The act of comparing
the two poems helps us to clarify the ways in which the worlds of
hawk and otter are psychologically differentiated. Only at the level
of the largest generalisation would it suffice to call these 'nature'
poems: the further we read into them the more we want to qualify
what, in this case, we mean when we use the word 'nature'.

A new and authentic poetic voice cannot be predicted. In the
later nineteen-fifties it did not seem likely that the world of nature
would provide a fruitful source of poetic inspiration. One would

have said that this territory had already been over-occupied and over-cultivated, particularly by English poets. And yet Ted Hughes is certainly a poet of the observable English landscape, who also in his verse makes use of the English alliterative tradition. Hughes's distinction derives from the freshness and sharpness of his psychological penetration of the features of that landscape, bringing them very close to us while at the same time showing us the distance between us and that landscape.

Even if new poems remain unpredictable, the poet's choice of subject matter is not wholly arbitrary. The poet draws on the work of earlier poets, and a new poem gathers in older strands and echoes, altering our view of what has gone before. Clearly there is an affinity between these poems and the animal poems of D. H. Lawrence which express the poet's fascination with the exotic strangeness of animal life. Nearer our own time, with its recent history of total war and the continuing shadowy threat of global destruction, is the work of Sidney Keyes who was killed during the war. *Hawk Roosting* owes something to Keyes's poem on the buzzard in the adoption of the bird's point of view as a way of focusing the poem. Keyes expressed admiration for the work of the early twentieth-century German poet, Rainer Maria Rilke, whose verse is often expressive of a preoccupation with animal energies, violence and death. The echoes of Rilke's poem on the panther in Hughes's *Jaguar* may not be conscious, but they are there. None of the foregoing, however, qualifies the poet's originality, it merely establishes the set of allegiances, the tradition that the poet's work itself makes.

In tones of uncompromising harshness, the hawk in *Hawk Roosting* proclaims its confident view of the world. Its language is direct, grammatically compressed and abrupt. The words do not flow; the broken rhythms force us rather than persuade us to attend. These and the hard consonants which support them prevent us from reading the poem as a lyric. Yet the mood of the first three stanzas is rhapsodic ('The convenience of the high trees!'), full of a sense of freedom and fierce energy in repose as the bird from its high perch celebrates its mode of life. The hawk is the lord of creation justified in its view because it is a perfectly adjusted instrument. Head and foot are shaped alike and there is complete continuity between sleeping and waking. The rhapsodic mood is broken by the interruption of the three terse lines in the fourth stanza when the hawk declares its unambiguous purpose.

This simplicity and clarity of a complete adaptation is, I think, the attraction of the subject matter to both poet and reader. The question is whether the poem, presented in the particularly forceful form of the dramatic monologue, commands our unqualified assent. Is the world really like this? Despite the unreflected single vision, the hawk speaks with two voices. We gain not only its view of the world and its purpose ('I'm going to keep things like this'), but at the same time its consciousness (or the poet's perhaps) of just how alien its view is to any human view of things. The hawk has no falsifying dream, no sophistry, no arguments, no manners. Like a totalitarian dictator ('the *whole* of Creation', 'it is *all* mine', 'the *one* path') it inhabits a world of only one dimension in which, although it can kill as it pleases, there are no real choices or alternatives, and in which things can never be other than they are, never be better. All that is dismissed as sophistry and falsification by the hawk is essential to the human condition. The bird in its extreme hostility to it reminds us that the world of human values exists.

Furthermore, in the grimly laconic final line of the poem the hawk tells us something about those human values. The line tells us that the world of the bird, and of the sun and the natural elements, is unchangeable. In so far as the hawk is the product of evolution, it is also its victim in a way in which human beings are not. For, central to human consciousness is the notion of change, the sense that things could be other than they are in a world where genuine choices exist.

Nevertheless, by its implications and resonances, the poem forcibly reminds us that we may not ignore the indifferent pressures of evolution and the non-moral energies of nature. It also renews and sharpens our view of nature. Nature in this poem is not benign, not sympathetic to man's yearnings for permanent and absolute certainties. The certainties which the hawk displays are unscrupulous and violent.

An Otter. The dual nature of the otter is proverbial.

> *Falstaff:* What beast? why, an otter.
> *Prince:* An otter, Sir John! Why an otter?
> *Falstaff:* Why? she's neither fish nor flesh, a man know not where
> to have her.

(*Henry IV*, pt 1, III iii 124)

If the hawk is unambiguous and alien, then at least by analogy ('like a king in hiding') the otter in this poem is nearer human kind. In the description of the animal in part I, the language is more musical in the repetition of liquid or soft consonants. The arrangement of recurring vowel sounds moving through half-rhyme to rhyme echoes the English alliterative tradition as it has been modulated by earlier poets such as Gerard Manley Hopkins, Wilfred Owen and Dylan Thomas. This consciousness of an ancient lineage also attaches to the subject matter of the poem. The otter brings its own legend of ancient dispossession as, against the flow, it searches for its source or origin in an attempt to resolve the ambiguity of its nature. The otter also mourns for what it has lost ('crying to the old shape of the starlit land'). Further, the otter is an image of rootlessness. It is driven to adopt guerrilla tactics to survive against the odds of hounds and sticks in a world which has become alien to it. So, in the poem, the otter is at once contemporary and ancient in a way which is immediately recognisable as appropriate not only to the ostensible subject matter of the poem, but also to what is implied by it. The poem gains a tension and a vitality from this recognition, even though it seems to me that in stanza four the poet is in danger of losing the poem in a set of ready-made associations. 'King in hiding', 'bats go round', 'light and birdsong', 'walloping' and milk wagons do not measure up to the earlier, taut description. The return of daylight to such a landscape could, of itself, scarcely trouble the otter or deflect it from its self-imposed task. Its odyssey has been posed in more serious terms than those of a nostalgia for an irretrievable pastoral life ('sunken farms').

Although the two parts of the poem balance in that there are four stanzas of five lines followed by five of four lines, the mood changes dramatically in part II. The otter is now pursued and stands all but submerged in the shallows, waiting motionless, disciplined in every nerve and muscle, for the threat to pass. Its acute senses identify and discriminate the scents of danger in the air it must breathe. Survival depends on a strategy utterly foreign to human beings in that the otter will only survive by not expressing a self. It must rigorously deny the self which lies not in, but under the eyes, below the surface where the hunted otter must wait it out. Patience is too moral, too consciously human an activity to describe this endurance. So, the self is 'attendant'; that is, not only held in abeyance but subservient and secondary. There are limits to how far we as readers can feel with and not simply for the otter. The poet refuses to humanise the victim because human beings, with their hunting dogs and vermin-poles, are part of the hostility of the environment. The roots of the otter's existence and of its way of life are purely physical and unified ('blood is the belly of logic') despite the paradox of the duality and ambiguity of that existence. Its habit is to linger nowhere for fear of betrayal, and to make the most of its moments, yet it is well adapted to remain submerged and motionless in water. Its heart is well protected just as the otter itself is protected or camouflaged by the glassy surface of the water.

The last two lines shock us into distancing ourselves again from the otter. They are snapshots of man's violence which remove us from the temptation to sentimentalise our relationship with the animal, and claim an intimacy or sympathy with it which it would not understand. I have written that the otter is nearer than the hawk to human kind. Its search is towards roots in nature which would resolve the ambiguities of its divided existence. In this way the amphibian otter becomes an admirable image of man himself, cut off from roots within nature and from the full natural life of the senses.

Even when one sometimes feels that its pre-occupation with the themes of hostility and violence is a narrowing one, Ted Hughes's verse is an arresting and penetrating renewal of an ancient vision of life.

For further reading, these poems by Hughes might be considered next: *Pike*, *The Jaguar* and *Macaw and Little Miss*.

ROBERT GRAVES
Counting the Beats
End of Play

Commentary by Sydney Bolt

Counting the Beats

You, love, and I,
(He whispers) you and I,
And if no more than only you and I
What care you or I?

5   Counting the beats,
Counting the slow heart beats,
The bleeding to death of time in slow heart beats,
Wakeful they lie.

Cloudless day,
10   Night, and a cloudless day,
Yet the huge storm will burst upon their heads one day
From a bitter sky.

Where shall we be,
(She whispers) where shall we be,
15   When death strikes home, O where then shall we be
Who were you and I?

Not there but here,
(He whispers) only here,
As we are, here, together, now and here,
20   Always you and I.

Counting the beats,
Counting the slow heart beats,
The bleeding to death of time in slow heart beats,
Wakeful they lie.

End of Play

We have reached the end of pastime, for always,
Ourselves and everyone, though few confess it
Or see the sky other than, as of old,
A foolish smiling Mary-mantle blue;

5   *Though life may still seem to dawdle golden*
       In some June landscape among giant flowers,
       The grass to shine as cruelly green as ever,
       Faith to descend in a chariot from the sky—

       May seem only: a mirror and an echo
10   *Mediate henceforth with vision and sound.*
       The cry of faith, no longer mettlesome,
       Sounds as a blind man's pitiful plea of 'blind'.

       We have at last ceased idling, which to regret
       Were as shallow as to ask our milk-teeth back;
15   *As many forthwith do, and on their knees*
       Call lugubriously upon chaste Christ.

       We tell no lies now, at last cannot be
       The rogues we were—so evilly linked in sense
       With what we scrutinized that lion or tiger
20   *Could leap from every copse, strike and devour us.*

       No more shall love in hypocrite pomp
       Conduct its innocents through a dance of shame,
       From timid touching of gloved fingers
       To frantic laceration of naked breasts.

25   *Yet love survives, the word carved on a sill*
       Under antique dread of the headsman's axe;
       It is the echoing mind, as in the mirror
       We stare on our dazed trunks at the block kneeling.

The ancient tradition of love poetry is almost dead. Admittedly, modern love poets do write poems dealing with the amorous relationships of men and women, but that is a different matter. The relationship as they present it is a comparatively limited one. While it may involve suffering, it no longer involves the overwhelming sense, characteristic of earlier love poetry, that nothing else matters. The contemporary poet cannot bring himself to claim that his whole life is centred in another individual. He is too keenly aware of the psychological facts neatly summarised in the second line of a poem by W. H. Auden—

        Lay your sleeping head, my love,
        Human on my faithless arm.

No woman can ever be, in the full sense of the word, his 'mistress'.

Without a mistress the typical Renaissance poet would have been without a theme. According to Robert Graves, the case is much the same with the typical modern poet who, casting around for subject matter, trespasses into areas where he usually has no right to be, and, pretending to be at home there, is guilty of 'vulgarity'. 'Every theatrical impersonation, every political, theological, or philosophical handout passed off as his own, is a vulgarity.' The first prophylactic which he recommends to poets against vulgarity is 'always to be in love'. Certainly love has been his principal, if not his only, theme for more than half a century.

Nothing could be more conventional than the manifest, paraphrasable content of *Counting the Beats*. Two lovers, whispers, heart beats, the sky, a storm, death pictured as a blow—the imagery is stereotyped. And if the diction is unusual, its originality lies not in its range but in its simplicity. 'O where then shall we be/Who were you and I?' reads like an attempt to translate an adult thought into baby-talk. The theme, also, is conventional. Of course, this does not mean that the poem is shallow. The need to establish a connection between death and erotic love lies somewhere very deep in human nature. But taken at its face value, the statement 'Always you and I' sounds more like a vain protest against death's supremacy than a valid claim to supremacy over death.

That is not how the words sound *in the poem*. The face value of the words is so enhanced by the movement of the verse that, by the time the claim 'Always you and I' is made, it is entirely convincing. The poem is a superb example of the way in which by adding an extra dimension to the meaning of words, versification can be convincing in itself.

As the title suggests, beats are the life and soul of this poem. A sensitive reading of the second stanza makes this clear. Consider the second line—'Counting the slow heart beats'. A normal speech rendering distributes the stresses as follows: 'COUNTING the SLOW HEART beats'. (We normally say 'heart beats' as we say 'oil-cloth' or 'first-fruits', placing a stress on the first syllable, despite the equal weight of the second.) In this case, however, the stanza form requires us to match the second line with the first, and in the first line the word 'beats' carries a natural stress—'COUNTing the BEATS'. We therefore give a matching (but unnatural) stress to the same word when it occurs at the end of the second line. This distortion of natural speech is not, of course, an arbitrary imposition. On the contrary, it expresses the meaning of the words—'slow heart beats'. As each word is now equally stressed, the result is three distinct thuds, three countable beats.

The second stanza also introduces a metrical feature which dominates the poem from then on. 'COUNTing the BEATS', 'COUNTing the SLOW', 'BLEEDing to DEATH', WAKEful they LIE'—each of these phrases has the same metrical structure: DUM-di-di-DUM. This structure is read as a single pattern, because it is the most prominently repeated metrical feature of the poem. If the poem presented a repeated pattern of disyllabic feet, it would be read as a trochee (DUM-di) followed by an iamb (di-DUM), as we read the first four syllables of the iambic line—'When to the sessions of sweet silent thought'. In this poem, however, there is no repeated pattern of disyllabic feet. The most prominent metrical feature is the recurrence of the structure exhibited in its title—'Counting the beats'. This is, in fact, a classical metrical foot, rare in English verse, called a 'choriamb'.

The second stanza fixes the choriamb in the reader's mind, so that in subsequent stanzas, feeling how the verse 'goes', he finds it again and again—in *'night* and a *cloud'* in line 10, for example, and even (suppressing the stress he might have given to 'huge') in *'yet* the huge *storm'.* The final stanza, by repeating this metrical key, clinches its dominance, which consequently extends itself in subsequent readings, as for example in the poem's opening line. The only stanza which resists this process is the fifth. Here the lines have an irrepressibly rising rhythm. Even when it is merely whispered, 'Not *there*/but *here'* does not give way to *'not* there but *here'* which is totally incongruous (with its suggestion of an irritated direction to an unobservant person trying to find something). The recalcitrance of this stanza, which contains the lover's words of reassurance, is highly expressive. The failure of the choriamb to impose itself expresses, rhythmically, the failure of death to impose itself. This effect, however, is subsidiary to the dramatic use which is made of the choriamb through the poem.

Unobtrusively, but none the less noticeably, the versification imposes slight distortions of natural speech stress which are not arbitrary but significant. We have already seen how this operates in the case of the line—'Counting the slow heart beats'—where the beats are made to come slow. More generally the attempt to impose the choriamb on the syllables has the same effect. It was the line— 'Counting the beats'—which unmistakeably announced the dominance of the choriamb. Its effect is, precisely, to make the reader count beats as he reads. If the placing of stresses, which is normally an unconscious process, now becomes conscious, it has been transformed in just the same way that the lover's heart-beats have been transformed. We are not normally conscious of the beat of our hearts. When we do become conscious of it, the heart becomes a reminder of death, because we know that it will stop some day, and when it does so time will have come to an end for us. In this way the choriamb, made ominous by its association with the second stanza, extends the consciousness of bleeding to death throughout the poem. It is no figure of speech, but a literal description of what is happening rhythmically, to say that the lovers are bleeding to death throughout the poem. Their wakefulness is the proof of their consciousness of this process. And, by the same token, the heart has become a symbol of death, a remarkable transformation, simple yet original. (An interesting comparison can be made with these lines from Henry King's *The Exequy*.

> *But hark! My Pulse like a soft Drum*
> *Beats my approach, tells* Thee *I come.*

The comparison even extends to the metrical construction of the second of these two lines—two choriambs.)

And yet, although it is in this poem a symbol of death, the heart remains as ever a symbol of love. Such is the intimacy of the scene that the lovers cannot be imagined as each hypochondriacally counting his or her own heart beats in separation from the other. They are too close. They feel each other's heart-beats, and the threat which sounds in their heart-beats is thus feared as a threat to their relationship, not as a threat to each individually. This is what justifies the man's reply to the woman's question.

The stanza form is conducive to the same effect. In each stanza the first three lines all end with the same word, and this repetition is the mark of the relationship of the meanings of these lines. The meaning of the first line is not developed in the lines which succeed it, but merely expanded. Each line, in fact, is merely an expansion of its predecessor.

> No there but here,
> (He whispers) only here,
> As we are, here, together, now and here,
> Always you and I.

The only exception to this construction is the third stanza, where there is a shift from cloudlessness (in the present) to a storm (in the future). This is the only stanza which is about something to come. The other stanzas all stand still in the immediate present, fixed at a point of recognition beyond which it seems impossible to advance. This, clearly, is an appropriate form to give to the moment of death, repeatedly sounded in the choriamb. And yet, what is expressed in each of these stanzas is love. It is for this reason that the line—'Always you and I'—does not sound like an empty protest. It enacts its meaning. The poem therefore demonstrates, even though it may not prove, that the moments of love and death can be identical.

In reconfirming an ancient theme which most contemporary poets neglect, *Counting the Beats* is typical of Graves's work. Typical also is the way in which it frames an immediate experience, the lovers' absorption in each other, by relating it to an expectation of catastrophe, in this case death. The expectation of catastrophe is central to Graves's view of life, which seems to have been formed in the trenches of the 1914-18 war, and had developed, by 1948, into a quasi-religious tragic philosophy proclaimed as belief in a 'White Goddess', whom all men (but especially poets) must serve, even though the role imposed upon them by such service was that of victim. The inevitable catastrophe which constitutes the tragedy of human—and more especially masculine—life is not, however, death, but something which happens again and again in the course of one man's life, so that by learning from his experience he can come to accept his fate, and thus transcend it. This acceptance of a cruel fate is the 'end of play', the beginning of serious adult life.

The significance of the words of *End of Play* is not, as in *Counting the Beats* obvious. Part of the difficulty is due to the admirable compression with which Graves—a more intellectual poet than is sometimes realised—diagnoses states of mind, most notably in—

> *so evilly linked in sense*
> *With what we scrutinised that lion or tiger*
> *Could leap from every copse, strike and devour us.*

In this connection it is worth observing that he was probably the first English poet to grasp the theories of psychoanalysis so intimately that they contributed to his natural mental processes. These lines describe the psychological mechanism known as 'projection'. 'The most striking characteristic of symptom-formation in paranoia', wrote Freud,* 'is the process which deserves the name of *projection*. An internal perception is suppressed, and, instead, its content, after undergoing a certain degree of distortion, enters consciousness in the form of an external perception.' In other words, troublesome desires cause us to see things 'which are not there', thus giving external objects (including other people) irrational power over us. The image of seeing a tiger in a copse, where in reality no tiger can possibly be, is a diagrammatically clear presentation of this process. The word 'sense', in the phrase 'linked in sense', is significantly ambiguous. Our senses betray us, when we see something which is not there. We are significantly linked with external objects when we interpret them subjectively, so that the word 'sense' here also means 'meaning'. Further compression results from the reader's being left to see for himself the link between these lines and the next stanza. As two lovers come to see each other as they really are, instead of as they had imagined each other to be, their relationship becomes a 'dance of shame'. This will no longer happen to a lover who has freed himself from this process.

* *Psycho-Analytic Notes upon an Autobiographical Account of a Case of Paranoia.* In *Sick Love*, Graves introduces 'the paranoiac fury' as one of the monsters, 'in outer blackness', threatening love as it proceeds along 'the heavenly causeway'.

A further source of difficulty is the way in which the words contradict each other. The general tenor of the poem is that experience brings realism, which frees us from unjustified extravagance of feeling. In the poem *Never Such Love*, Graves ironically records the absolute terms in which lovers describe their mutual passion. To preserve the proclamation made in this poem from similar irony he substitutes (at the cost of some confusion of the reader) the phrase 'for always' for the phrase 'for ever', with its extravagant overtones. And yet the emotional exaggeration which he seems to be condemning is present in the poem, despite such precautions. Thus, while it is not himself but those who do not share his vision whom he characterises as 'lugubrious', he is so insistent that beauty is cruel that 'cruelly green' is inappropriately applied to the grass as it appears *before*, as well as after, the recognition of what he regards as the bitter truth about life.

Contradictions of this kind, however, are only expressions of the inner tension which lies at the heart of the poem, and gives it life. Love is recognised as doomed, inevitably proceeding 'from timid touching of gloved fingers' to its opposite, 'frantic laceration of naked breasts'. But it survives this recognition. If it is infantile to expect love to be happy, it is no less infantile, it is unmanly, to refuse to love because love is doomed. The poet does not claim to be invulnerable to passion. He still feels it, but now his vulnerability is modified by reflection ('a mirror'), and memory ('an echo'). And when love turns to hate he will no longer be ashamed because he is no longer an 'innocent'. He knows now, when he falls in love, that he is laying his head upon a block, and that the fall of the axe will surely come. Reflection and memory, indeed, enable him to anticipate its stroke, so that he sees in advance his trunk, headless.

The fact that the subject of the poem is sexual love is, of course, a further source of difficulty, because at first reading the subject seems to be much broader, namely a total view of life. The sixth stanza is the only place where sexual love is obviously the subject, and it might well seem to be introduced there merely as one example, one field of many, where pessimistic realism is preferable to religious faith. (This poem was published in 1938, ten years before *The White Goddess*.) The references to a 'Mary-mantle blue' sky in the first stanza, 'Faith . . . in a chariot from the sky' in the second, the cry of faith in the third, and the invocation of Christ in the fourth, all suggest that 'the end of pastime' means the abandonment of religious consolation. Such a reading would be superficial. A close reading, alive to implications, shows that Christianity is under consideration only as an attitude to love, a subject on which its guidance is regarded as pointless because Christ was chaste and Mary a virgin.

It is at this point—its manner of dismissing Christianity—that the difficulty of the poem is a sign of the limitation in it, because that dismissal is, to borrow the poet's own word, so shallow. It is no criticism of the poem to point out that Christianity is dismissed merely because its guidance in the matter of love is found inadequate. If Graves considers religion only in this one aspect, his restriction of attitude is due to the fact that he regards the relationship of man and woman as the essential relationship of human life. For him there is no distinction between a total attitude to life and an attitude to love. Whether or not he concurs in this identification, the reader who wishes to receive what the poem has to offer is ready to accept it for purposes of reading and understanding. And in the same way, as a reader, he should be prepared, even if he is a Christian, to entertain the possibility of rejecting Christianity. But even if he is not Christian he cannot accept a rejection of Christianity so arbitrary—it could even be said so vulgar—as this. It is clearly perverse to describe the desire to recover lost faith as a desire to recover teeth of any kind, naïve not to realise that a faith which sounded mettlesome would be suspect, and obtuse to offer as pejorative an image of faith (as a blind beggar) which would be welcome to the faithful. Over and above all these particular points, however, stands the general argumentative point that Christianity 'mediates' sexual passion not by an insistence upon 'innocence' but by the sacrament of marriage, which the poem completely ignores.

It is here that the poem founders, on the question of the quality of the relationship it deals with. To put the point briefly, it equates love with infatuation. There is, no doubt, an element of infatuation in the process of falling in love. Married love survives the disappearance of this element. For Graves, however, its disappearance marks the beginning of alienation, and is therefore fatal. For him the heroic persistence in loving which he proclaims in the poem means the ability to fall in and out of love over and over again with different women, knowing all the time, in each case, that love will not last. Love of this description is merely compulsive behaviour characterised by a plain streak of masochism. While insisting that all poetry is essentially love poetry, he also tells us (in the introduction to *Collected Poems, 1968*) that 'My main theme was always the practical impossibility, transcended only by a belief in miracle, of absolute love continuing between man and woman'. Adoption of such an attitude must appear as the abandonment of serious emotion, the beginning rather than the end of 'play'. It is not a responsible attitude, but a wilful one.

It is not just to reflection that this wilfulness reveals itself. It makes itself felt in the poem, in its expression. There is a continuous attempt to inject into the reader a response which does not arise naturally. Why, for example, are we 'rogues' when we project our feelings upon external objects? (The word 'rogues', with its association of vagabond mischief is peculiarly inappropriate.) Why is the process 'evil'? Why is the word 'foolish' employed in line 4, and 'shallow' in line 14? We are not invited to share a feeling; we are told what to feel. Even more insistently, by the use of the pronoun 'we' in the first, fourth and fifth stanzas, we are told that we do already feel it. Together with this bullying, and especially when the word 'we' is used, goes a brutal assertiveness in the verbal movement—

We have reached the end of pastime, for always, . . .

We have at least ceased idling . . .

We tell no lies now . . .

(In parenthesis, it is also to be remarked how sensitively texture is used to reinforce meaning, as for example in 'dawdle golden', and in the contrast of 'timid touching' with 'frantic laceration'.)

Wilfulness also reveals itself in the final image, in which the poem reaches a climax contrived both by syntax and rhythm, both indicating that a turning-point has been reached with the opening of the final stanza. The image is forceful, even unforgettable. It is, however, melodramatic rather than dramatic. Its sensationalism exceeds its significance, for, in fact, this execution is only one of a string of similar operations, the breaking off of another affair for which, possibly, a visit to the dentist might have been an apter image. But even if it stood for the end of the love of a lifetime, the image of the condemned man on the scaffold might still seem too posed, the posture in which it involved the poet too theatrical. It converts personal loss into a public spectacle.

In conclusion it should be noted that the introduction of the White Goddess has rescued Graves' love poems from two of the pitfalls into which *End of Play* falls. As the poems are written for the Goddess, not for a human reader, no attempt is made in these later poems to impose eccentric attitudes upon the reader, while the readiness to be enchanted by women for a necessarily brief period seems less feeble when it is represented as part of a religious cult.

The reader new to Robert Graves might proceed to read: *Love Without Hope, The Cool Web, The Castle, Sick Love, Never Such Love, The Great Grandmother.*

The above poems precede publication of *The White Goddess* (1948). Poems written after that date include *The Survivor, Cry Faugh!, The Blue-Fly, Call It a Good Marriage, The Quiet Glades of Eden, The Hung Wu Vase.*

PHILIP LARKIN
Church Going
Wedding Wind

Commentary by Keith Sagar

Church Going

Once I am sure there's nothing going on
I step inside, letting the door thud shut.
Another church: matting, seats, and stone,
And little books; sprawlings of flowers, cut
5   For Sunday, brownish now; some brass and stuff
Up at the holy end; the small neat organ;
And a tense, musty, unignorable silence,
Brewed God knows how long. Hatless, I take off
My cycle-clips in awkward reverence,

10   Move forward, run my hand around the font.
From where I stand, the roof looks almost new—
Cleaned, or restored? Someone would know: I don't.
Mounting the lectern, I peruse a few
Hectoring large-scale verses, and pronounce
15   'Here endeth' much more loudly than I'd meant.
The echoes snigger briefly. Back at the door
I sign the book, donate an Irish sixpence,
Reflect the place was not worth stopping for.

Yet stop I did: in fact I often do,
20   And always end much at a loss like this,
Wondering what to look for; wondering, too,
When churches fall completely out of use
What we shall turn them into, if we shall keep
A few cathedrals chronically on show,
25   Their parchment, plate and pyx in locked cases,
And let the rest rent-free to rain and sheep.
Shall we avoid them as unlucky places?

Or, after dark, will dubious women come
To make their children touch a particular stone;
30   Pick simples for a cancer; or on some
Advised night see walking a dead one?
Power of some sort or other will go on
In games, in riddles, seemingly at random;

But superstition, like belief, must die,
35 And what remains when disbelief has gone?
Grass, weedy pavement, brambles, buttress, sky,

A shape less recognisable each week,
A purpose more obscure. I wonder who
Will be the last, the very last, to seek
40 This place for what it was; one of the crew
That tap and jot and know what rood-lofts were?
Some ruin-bibber, randy for antique,
Or Christmas-addict, counting on a whiff
Of gown-and-bands and organ-pipes and myrrh?

45 Or will he be my representative,
Bored, uninformed, knowing the ghostly silt
Dispersed, yet tending to this cross of ground
Through suburb scrub because it held unspilt
So long and equably what since is found
50 Only in separation—marriage, and birth,
And death, and thoughts of these—for whom was built
This special shell? For, though I've no idea
What this accoutred frowsty barn is worth,
It pleases me to stand in silence here;

55 A serious house on serious earth it is,
In whose blent air all our compulsions meet,
Are recognised, and robed as destinies.
And that much never can be obsolete,
Since someone will forever be surprising
60 A hunger in himself to be more serious,
And gravitating with it to this ground,
Which, he once heard, was proper to grow wise in,
If only that so many dead lie round.

Wedding Wind

The wind blew all my wedding-day.
And my wedding-night was the night of the high wind;
And a stable door was banging, again and again,
That he must go and shut it, leaving me

Stupid in candlelight, hearing rain,
Seeing my face in the twisted candlestick,
Yet seeing nothing. When he came back
He said the horses were restless, and I was sad
That any man or beast that night should lack
10   *The happiness I had.*

                    Now in the day
All's ravelled under the sun by the wind's blowing.
He has gone to look at the floods, and I
Carry a chipped pail to the chicken-run,
15   *Set it down, and stare. All is the wind*
Hunting through clouds and forests, thrashing
My apron and the hanging cloths on the line.
Can it be borne, this bodying forth by wind
Of joy my actions turn on, like a thread
20   *Carrying beads? Shall I be let to sleep*
Now this perpetual morning shares my bed?
Can even death dry up
These new delighted lakes, conclude
Our kneeling as cattle by all-generous waters?

If one were to ask the average critic, well up in contemporary poetry, what sort of poetry Philip Larkin writes, one would be told, I think, that it is mundane, flat, self-deprecatory; that he has an eye for telling details of contemporary life, something in the manner of Betjeman; that his largest and commonest themes are frustration and death—a hopeful future quickly turning into a sour, uneventful present, a threadbare past,

                    And age, and then the only end of age;

that he is a valetudinarian, tenderly nursing, in Charles Tomlinson's phrase, his sense of defeat. A number of poems would be cited to support this view: *Next Please, No Road, Toads, I Remember I Remember, Mr Bleaney, As Bad As a Mile, Ambulances, Dockery and Son, Reference Back, Essential Beauty, Send No Money, Afternoons* . . . Quite a large number, one might say. Yet it is always dangerous to generalise. Ted Hughes writes about animals, we used to be told. So we read his animal poems as though they were *only* about animals; and we skipped the poems with no animals in them. Some of the Larkin poems I have listed are fine, but he has written other and very different poems which our fixed expectations can easily prevent us from recognising.

Larkin's work came to my attention when a handful of his poems appeared in *New Lines*, an anthology edited by Robert Conquest, in 1956. In making his selection for *New Lines* Conquest sought to present what he took to be the significant characteristics of the poetry of the 'fifties in reaction against the pretentiousness of the 'forties, whether the heady self-and-nature celebrating of Dylan Thomas or T. S. Eliot's wrestling with words and meanings and the last things at a great height. The 'fifties poets, Conquest claimed, were 'down to earth', rooted in common experience with a reverence for the real person or event; men speaking to men in a manner in which they could hope to be generally understood about matters human and humane and rational. These are, I think, real virtues, and the reaction was necessary. But in fact many of the poems chosen were not rooted in experiences we could feel to be important; they were commonplace, common men speaking of common things to common men all congratulating each other on their refusal to be taken in, aggressively provincial and slangy, disenchanted and deflated to the point of affectation . . . Most disabling of all was the refusal to handle or even acknowledge a whole dimension of human experience beyond the merely local and day-to-day to which poetry has traditionally striven to find access. In the words of Charles Tomlinson: 'They show a singular want of vital awareness of the continuum outside themselves, of the mystery embodied over against them in the created universe' (*Essays in Criticism*, April 1957). The anthology, he concluded, testified to 'a total failure of nerve'. (It is worth noting that the work of Ted Hughes was not represented.)

Such reservations were widely felt and voiced. They were applied to Larkin just as much as to Kingsley Amis, and it seems that many critics got into their heads at that time a fixed idea about the kind of poet Larkin is which they have never got out again.

What we first become aware of as we begin to read *Church Going* is a tone of voice, ordinary, conversational, casual, perfectly fitting the speaker, this mild bore who has left his bicycle propped against a gravestone. He enters the church only when 'there's nothing going on'; the building itself is undistinguished, just 'another church' in another suburb. He neither knows nor cares about churches, their accoutrements, the acts of worship which take place there, the faith they serve. His attitude is, if not quite disrespectful, at least flippant.

The poem is dramatic in that the meaning depends upon a relationship between the subject matter and the voice speaking. In some poems (*A study of Reading Habits* for example) there is the adoption of a persona, a voice not the poet's 'true' voice. Here the assumed voice is the true voice of a part of himself, or of himself in his moments of smallness and commonness.

There seems to be a complete refusal of the 'poetical' in language, rhythm, subject matter. Yet our attention is held; we are committed to go on reading, particularly if we are reading aloud, by a verse movement so deftly organised that it draws no attention to itself, but, slowly, as the poem progresses, gathers momentum and dignity. The language too begins unostentatiously to accumulate reserves of power. Notice, for example, how the stale, wry 'brewed' of the first stanza modulates into the fresh 'blent' of the last.

Just as, in the verse, we have considerable technical skill passing itself off as casualness, so the speaker attempts to assert his philistinism, his not being taken in—'some brass and stuff/Up at the holy end'—yet cannot help noticing the neatness of the small organ, cannot ignore the silence, cannot keep God altogether out of it, even if the reference is flippant, cannot, that is, avoid a response of 'awkward reverence' to the ambience of the place.

The comedy is not at all at the expense of the church, but of the speaker, whose clumsy attempts at mockery are protests against whatever it is that demands reverence from a man to whom Christianity means nothing. His pronouncing of 'Here endeth' is a gesture against the silence which he would rather ignore or break; but the gesture rebounds, the silence wins, quickly stifling the sniggering echo. It seems impervious to time, change or intrusion.

The beginning of the third stanza signals a change of tone. This man who had seemed a shallow clown is driven to analyse the power which drew him here and has often drawn him to such places. Gradually he takes on a representative function, the spokesman of all of us who cannot approach churches in a spirit of piety and faith, yet visit them and find some need obscurely satisfied. As the enquiry deepens in seriousness, the speaker finds new resources of language and hence of insight. The man who donated the Irish sixpence is now pleased to stand in silence and be serious, and we feel that the transformation has been brought about by the church. The point and power of the poem lies in the fact that this utterly undistinguished individual is shown to be capable of 'surprising a hunger in himself to be more serious', and that particular cross of ground to be capable of eliciting such a hunger in any chance passer-by. The timeless silence of the church and the presence of so many dead combine to displace even the most cynical and small-minded churchgoer, to nudge him gently to one side of himself—the self which makes cracks, the self entirely caught up in the world of compulsions—the compulsion to get up and go to work and spend and turn the television on; the compulsion to be born, to copulate, to die. From this vantage point these naked compulsions 'Are recognised, and robed as destinies'.

Larkin is thinking, of course, of the three great Christian ceremonies, christening, wedding, funeral, which, whether we regard them as sacramental or not, ritualise the great crises of human experience, give them form and dignity and recognition as constituting not the fortuitous experiences of individuals helpless and naked in a world of obscurely felt compulsions, but the essential framework or rhythm of all human experience. This destiny is recognised whenever a man is forced to see his own life as part of the continuity of the race, over and above the rise and decline of particular religions. And it is not something one simply has to come to terms with, to acquiesce in, but something from which one can draw strength and fulness of life.

Of course, there is no great original thought here. The power derives from the resources of language Larkin is able to draw on to embody these ideas. We hardly notice the change of tone as the poem progresses, but it is sufficient to put the poet in a position, by the sixth stanza, to exploit the full poetic resources of his language.

Look at the organisation of this sentence:

> Or will he be my representative,
> Bored, uninformed, knowing the ghostly silt
> Dispersed, yet tending to this cross of ground
> Through suburb scrub because it held unspilt
> So long and equably what since is found
> Only in separation—marriage, and birth,
> And death, and thoughts of these—for whom was built
> This special shell?

In speaking these lines aloud, the voice follows a perfect parabola. The rhythm lifts the voice to the word 'unspilt', accumulating emphasis, then holds the climax for four more words before falling away. The liquid sound of the word 'equably', taken in conjunction with 'unspilt', strongly suggests a brimming vessel with all its associations of benison and fruition.

We take it as given that the poem is written by an atheist. I take it as a most sensitive and gracious rendering of what a church has to offer to an atheist, and I believe that most Christian readers of the poem are able to take it in the same way.

That the image of the brimming cup is not, for Philip Larkin, factitious, is demonstrated conclusively by the delightful little poem *Water* (in *The Whitsun Weddings*), a poem such as Lawrence's *Pansies* were intended to be, but mostly failed for lack of technique.

Perhaps *Church Going* won its place in *New Lines* and its early reputation partly because of the fashionable tone of the opening stanzas. But, as we have seen, the enclosing tone is quite different, and exposes in the assumed comic persona those very limitations of sensibility, enthusiasm and tenderness which characterised *New Lines*.

Larkin's first collection of poems, *The North Ship*, was published in 1945. Many of the poems are about two worlds, the world of 'unfenced existence', a quick world of morning and sunshine, a clamour of birdsong, big winds blowing and

> the unguessed-at heart riding
> The winds as gulls do

and the 'unquickened world' of 'ashen hills' and 'salted, shrunken lakes', of dark streets, 'hurrying and troubled faces', loneliness, hopelessness and death; about the distance between these worlds and the difficulty or impossibility of bringing them into creative contact; about the rare, unforeseen moments when that contact is spontaneously made. The poignancy of the sad poems derives from this awareness of what is beyond reach for so many of us, and for all of us most of the time.

In *The North Ship* wind is the dominant image, standing for all the huge forces, creative and destructive, outside the merely human. It is joy and tragedy, that to which life is occasionally given over, including those forces normally locked in the unsuspected depths of our own being. It figures hardly at all in the later books, where there are more indoor poems, looking out through windows, avoiding exposure and risk. *Wedding Wind* is an outstanding exception, which adds a dimension to all the other poems in *The Less Deceived*.

Here Larkin adopts the persona of a newly married young woman. There is no sign in her of Larkin's own usual reticence and mildness. The opening lines typify the technical assurance of the whole poem, its strength of feeling and imagery:

> *The wind blew all my wedding-day,*
> *And my wedding-night was the night of the high wind;*

The same lovely simplicity and directness is everywhere apparent:

> *and I was sad*
> *That any man or beast that night should lack*
> *The happiness I had.*

The passion which sweeps through her carries away her former self, all her former thoughts and bearings, so that when the man leaves her she feels 'stupid' and does not recognise her own face in the twisted candlestick. But what she had mistaken for stupidity she later finds to be a new central reality of joy on which all her actions now turn 'like a thread carrying beads'. The wind 'bodies forth' this joy as it thrashes her apron and the hanging cloths on the line. Not only has the wind ravelled yesterday's world, it has released pent-up waters, transforming them into 'new delighted lakes', 'all generous waters'. The awakening of her capacity for love and wonder is marvellously conveyed:

> Shall I be let to sleep
> *Now this perpetual morning shares my bed?*

The great wind embodies what is, perhaps, only a temporary experience, but the 'all-generous waters' it has released are felt to be permanent, or permanently renewable.

The richly deployed imagery of wind and flood is not at all literary, but assumes, and triumphantly vindicates the assumption, that these primal images can still carry a great charge of controlled feeling when handled with sufficient delicacy and conviction. They enable Larkin here to achieve a unique blend of virginal innocence, frank sensuality and religious awe.

Larkin's stylistic achievement depends upon far more than technical mastery. The depth and subtlety of his response to language gives him access to the permanent realities of experience the language holds. As all true poets do, he makes words live; he makes us proud to share a language capable of such precision and splendour.

There are only three slim volumes of Larkin's poetry (see p. 192). The following anthologies offer several examples: *The New Poetry*, ed., A. Alvarez, Penguin 1962. *New Lines*, ed., R. Conquest, 1 and 2, Macmillan 1956, 1963. *Poetry 1900 to 1965*, ed., George MacBeth, Longmans 1967. Larkin has recorded *Mr Bleaney* and *An Arundel Tomb* from *The Whitsun Weddings* on JUR 00A8 while *Ambulances* and *Days* are read by Hugh Dickson on *Poetry 1900–1965* Longmans 34155.

Faced with so small an output there is really no excuse for not reading the whole of Larkin, but I should like to draw attention to a number of simple poems before which the critic can only stand dumbstruck with admiration: *Coming, Going, Age, Absences, Days, As Bad as a Mile, First Sight.*

DONALD DAVIE
Remembering the Thirties
Hornet
Low Lands

Commentary by John Lucas

Remembering the Thirties

I

Hearing one saga we enact the next.
We please our elders when we sit enthralled;
But then they're puzzled; and at last they're vexed
To have their youth so avidly recalled.

5   It dawns upon the veterans after all
That what for them were agonies, for us
Are high-brow thrillers, though historical;
And all their feats quite strictly fabulous.

This novel written fifteen years ago,
10   Set in my boyhood and my boyhood home,
These poems about 'abandoned workings', show
Worlds more remote than Ithaca or Rome.

The Anschluss, Guernica—all the names
At which the poets thrilled or were afraid
15   For me mean schools, and schoolmasters and games;
And in the process some-one is betrayed.

Ourselves perhaps. The Devil for a joke
Might carve his own initials on our desk,
And yet we'd miss the point because he spoke
20   An idiom too dated, Audenesque.

Ralegh's Guiana also killed his son.
A pretty pickle if we came to see
The tallest story really packed a gun,
The Telemachiad an Odyssey.

II

25   Even to them the tales were not so true
As not to be ridiculous as well:
The ironmaster met his Waterloo,
But Rider Haggard rode along the fell.

'Leave for Cape Wrath tonight!' They lounged away
30 On Fleming's trek or Isherwood's ascent.
England expected every man that day
To show his motives were ambivalent.

They played the fool, not to appear as fools
In time's long glass. A deprecating air
35 Disarmed, they thought, the jeers of later schools;
Yet irony itself is doctrinaire,

And, curiously, nothing now betrays
Their type to time's derision like this coy
Insistence on the quizzical, their craze
40 For showing Hector was a mother's boy.

A neutral tone is nowadays preferred.
And yet it may be better, if we must,
To find the stance impressive and absurd
Than not to see the hero for the dust.

45 For courage is the vegetable king,
The sprig of all ontologies, the weed
That beards the slag-heap with his hectoring,
Whose green adventure is to run to seed.

Hornet

In lilac trained on the colonnade's archway, what
Must be a hornet volleys lethally back
And forth in the air, on the still not hot
But blindingly white Italian stone, blue-black.

5 I have seldom seen them in England, although once
Years ago the foul-mouthed, obligingly bowed
Rat-catcher of Cambridge made a just pretence
To a cup of tea, for a nest cleared in the road.

Those were wasp-coloured, surely; and this blue,
10 Gun-metal blue, blue-black ominous ranger
Of Italy's air means an Italy stone all through,
Where every herb of holier thought's a stranger.

No call for such rage in our England of pierced shadows.
Stone's and the white sun's opposite, furious fly,
15 There no sun strides in a rapid creak of cicadas
And the green mould stains before the mortar is dry.

Low Lands

I could not live here, though I must and do
Ungratefully inhabit the Cambridgeshire fens,
And the low river delta we pass through
Is beautiful in the same uncertain sense.

5 Like a snake it is, its serpentine iridescence
Of slow light spilt and wheeling over calm
Inundations, and a snake's still menace
Hooding with bruised sky belfry and lonely farm.

The grasses wave on meadows fat with foison.
10 In granges, cellars, granaries, the rat
Runs sleek and lissom. Tedium, a poison,
Swells in the sac for the hillborn, dwelling in the flat.

How defenceless it is! How much it needs a protector
To keep its dykes! At what a price it commands
15 The delightful bizarre when it wears like a bus-conductor
Tickets of brown sails tucked into polder's hat-bands!

But a beauty there is, noble, dependent, unshrinking,
In being at somebody's mercy, wide and alone.
I imagine a hillborn sculptor suddenly thinking
20 One could live well in a country short of stone.

First impressions are general ones. In the case of *Remembering the Thirties* we are likely to be struck first of all by its trimness. It looks neat on the page and it reads neatly; the rhymes aim for exactness, the rhythms are unemphatic, the syntax is straightforward and the diction presents few difficulties, since it is very nearly stripped of imagery and puzzling locutions. In short, the style of this poem seems deliberately chaste and self-effacing. Such a style cannot be called negative, but we are likely to sense that it exists not for its own sake, but for the sake of the poem's argument. Of course, it takes considerable skill to write like this; and once the poet's decision about his style is taken there are many restraints he has to impose on himself. But the tactic is sound, for since we are aware of the pains the poet has taken to clear away obstacles to comprehension, we surely feel that he regards what he has to say as of real importance to himself and his readers; we recognize that his poem is a candid effort at communication and that we are therefore allowed to be in a very good position to judge its worth because of his care to make sure that we understand it.

But here a question may raise itself. If this poet is so interested in perspicuity, how are we to explain the presence of so many literary, historical and mythical allusions in his poem? Are not these proof of his wanting to persuade us of his cleverness, information, and fanciful ingenuity? And is not such a desire every bit as self-regarding as a peacock style? Such an objection must focus on each allusion in order to determine its propriety; and we may come to feel that some do not earn their keep. But it is also possible to argue that the poem's allusions are not there as evidence of the poet's self-regarding cleverness but as testimony to his desire to give his argument wide scope and authenticity. And by authenticity I mean that the poet's readiness to appeal to myth, literature and history is proof of the judicious thought that he has brought to bear on his subject, so that his poem is truly a considered statement and properly an act of wit (taking that word to mean what it did for Pope: an exercise of conceiving, judging and reasoning). Besides, the very fact that the poet makes such appeals is bound to elicit our active response; by putting all his cards on the table, as it were, he invites our agreement with what he has to say, and hence risks our disagreement. And surely much of the pleasure we take from this kind of poem has to do with our matching of wits against the poet's.

But what kind of a poem is *Remembering the Thirties*? The question is not easy to answer, for this poem does not readily accommodate itself to any of the genres into which we may be accustomed to try fitting poems. But we can perhaps come as near to its type as we need if we call it an exercise in ratiocination. It is a poem of reasoned statements; it progresses from judgments on a previous generation of writers through judgment about the poet himself and his contemporaries to speculative judgment about the nature of human commitment. But ratiocination must not be taken to mean that the poet's mind is 'made up' in any simple way. On the contrary, as the poem proceeds, so the poet's attitude to the writers of the 1930s becomes more complex. At first, he is near to regarding that generation of writers which had passionately involved itself in social and political issues as darling dodos. But by the end of the poem something altogether less dismissive is being said. And the saying of it implicates the poet in a manner that has moved a good way from his distanced attitude at the opening of the poem.

The first stanzas are controlled by a tone that hovers somewhere between amusement and contempt for their subject. The 'thirties writers are 'elders' and 'veterans' who tell of 'sagas'; the words are slightly tongue-in-cheek because all are to some degree archaic; they hint at magniloquence and suggest the 'strictly fabulous' feats of the second stanza. Moreover, the elders before whom 'we sit enthralled' are merely being milked for a good yarn; there is no question of their actually being believed. And that this is so 'dawns upon the veterans after all'. The line itself denies them serious treatment. The cliché 'dawns upon' mocks the veterans, suggesting that they are far from being mentally alert; and this is picked up by the words 'after all' (they ought to have guessed much earlier). It is as though the veterans, if not as fabulous as their feats, are certainly at a far remove from the nimble wits of their listeners; quaint old mastodons, in fact, put out to graze. Of course, this is to overstate, but after all we are condemned to the use of words which can at their best only approximate to the tone a poem releases, and as nearly as I can render it without repeating the poem's words, the tone of the opening stanzas of *Remembering the Thirties* is as I have described.

The next two stanzas go some way towards explaining the reason for this tone. The poet, we learn, grew up when and where the 'thirties writers were at work, and yet he cannot begin to connect their writing with any but trivial schoolboy experiences. I would note that a great deal of information is unobtrusively packed into these stanzas, and I would also note the way 'Ithaca or Rome' plays off against 'The Anschluss, Guernica'. The close of the third stanza and opening of the fourth make a neat rhetorical point of linking the recent to the ancient past which reduces them both to insignificance. What for the 'thirties writers had been the terrible annexing of Austria to Germany and the barbarous Nazi bombing of a defenceless Spanish town, for the poet are no more remarkable than scraps of memory that make up the boring routine of school.

And yet the very horror of what those names signify operates to trouble the tone that has governed the poem hitherto. The fifth and sixth stanzas, therefore, are compelled to move towards a sense of the reality that underlies those 'high-class thrillers'. The stanzas have something of self-judgment about them: 'we' may be the ones betrayed simply because we are too ready to be amused by the manner, not ready enough to be shocked by the matter. But self-judgment is played down, compromised by the deliberately 'vulgar' language of the last stanza. It is the middle lines that point the vulgarity:

> *A pretty pickle if we came to see*
> *The tallest story really packed a gun.*

The tone here is manifestly insensitive to the tragedy and heroism which the first and last lines tell of. And we are therefore made aware that the poet does not want to be knocked off his perch of superior amusement by the thought that, after all, the writers of the 1930s were engaged in tragic and perhaps even epic matters. And there is more to it than just that; for the references to Ralegh's son and Telemachus, the son of Ulysses, suggest that from generation to generation certain responsibilities are handed down. And we are therefore also made aware that the 'smart' language of the sixth stanza is a way of fending off a sense of inherited responsibility. 'A pretty pickle': putting it that way enables the poet to ward off the meaning that his own allusions to history and myth have generated. And we may add that because his language is so irresponsible it implies more self-judgment than anything that is overtly stated.

At this point the poem breaks away to fresh considerations. Even so, we are entitled to think the break suggestive of the poet's own uneasy conscience. And this is borne out by the way he reverts to pinning down the absurdities of the 'thirties writers.

> Even to them the tales were not so true
> As not to seem ridiculous as well.

I must note here that the writers the poet has in mind are Isherwood and the group which was once dubbed 'Macspaunday'; that is, Auden, Spender, MacNeice, Day Lewis. It excludes George Orwell, who saw nothing ridiculous in what he was fighting for or against. And I must also note the remarkable skill of the opening two stanzas of part II in their mimic rendering of the posture of Macspaunday. The joke at the end of the second stanza is exactly the sort of schoolboyish joke of which the group was so fond. And the first line of the second stanza wickedly hits off the group's characteristic note. 'Leave for Cape Wrath tonight.' The urgent cry takes added force from the trochee of the first foot and from the mythic Cape Wrath (just the sort of name Auden loved to invent). But it is then undercut by the phrase 'they lounged away', which not only demonstrates the group's unwillingness to be caught out in simple commitment but also hints that they were too well-bred for there to be much chance of that. ('Lounge' is a word with well-defined class associations: working-class boys may loiter, loll or slouch; but upper-class boys, as the Macspaunday group were, lounge.) Yet having commended the skill of these stanzas we need also to be aware that under them runs an uneasy conscience; it is as though the poet is saying 'don't blame me for not taking them seriously, they didn't do so themselves'. The tone of the last stanza of part I has sufficiently worried him to make an excuse necessary.

The excuse is broken down at the end of the poem, but before we come to that we have to deal with the two least satisfactory stanzas in the poem. There are several reasons for finding the third and fourth stanzas weak. In the first place, it is by no means certain that the group the poet is thinking of *did* want to guard against the jeers of later schools; in the second place, a deprecating air does not amount to irony; in the third place, the opening lines of the third stanza do not make sense (the image of time's long glass is really a careless cliché, and suggests the opposite of what is said, since if you play the fool in the glass you obviously will be seen doing so); and in the fourth place, though I accept that the Macspaunday group did indulge a 'quizzical' liking for showing that Hector was a mother's boy (and again, the poet has caught the very sort of example and phrasing dear to the group), I do not see the force of the word 'curiously,' because if irony is doctrinaire it is natural, not curious, that 'their type' should be betrayed by the quizzical.

If the third and fourth stanzas are the weakest in the poem, there is no doubt that the fifth and sixth are the most difficult. In the fifth stanza there is a real ambiguity about whose 'stance' is meant— Hector's or the writer's. The poet may be saying, well, at least they could see that Hector was a hero, or, let's admit that they were heroic even if absurd. In fact, I think the idea is that because they adopted an ironic stance, the 'thirties writers were able to write about heroism as 'we' are not; and therefore, it is implied, 'we' can not recognise their heroism as they recognised Hector's. This reading brings us back to the last stanza of part I, and it takes up the idea of guilty self-knowledge that had there been dropped. But we are left with this problem, that there seems no good reason why a neutral tone makes its user incapable of seeing the hero for the dust. After all, the refusal to recognise the heroic is made in stanza six of part I and that tone is not neutral. (I am also worried about why we 'must' decide between one or other attitude and rather suspect the word is there because it is the best the poet can do for his rhyme.) Thus the difficulties of the fifth stanza are not necessarily justifiable ones, but those of the sixth certainly are. This stanza is very finely written, and it noticeably moves away from the plain language of the rest of the poem to a complicated extended metaphor that does ample justice to the poet's own position and the idea of heroism. Courage, the poet says, is a sacrificial hero, a part-comic and part-celebratory idea; it is a 'vegetable king'. It is thus (so the implication of the unfolding metaphor insists) the sacred plant without which life itself is impossible— like the fabulous plants, haemony or moly. It is also a weed, a nuisance, because it acts as a rebuke to the common mass of men who do not want to be disturbed from their indifference by acts of heroism (so that 'weed' is a very ambiguous word). But if 'beards' means affronts, it also means covers, and the line therefore hints not only at the hero's (Hector's) reproof to complacency, but at the ability of the 'thirties writers to dignify the squalor of their age ('slag-heap' is a feature of the industrial landscape that plays a prominent part in much 'thirties writing). The last line of the poem says that it is really a law of the universe that heroism should play itself out, and that it is therefore natural behaviour (more natural than the sceptical amusement with which it is likely to be regarded). Thus in retrospect, even the mocked-at seediness of the 'veterans' has its natural propriety.

The last stanza of *Remembering the Thirties* brings the poem very finely to its close. Without losing hold of the wit that he has demonstrated throughout, the poet manages to move towards a juster and more generous appraisal of the idea of heroism than had seemed possible at the end of part I. There is no process of simplification involved here; indeed, it is the very intelligence of the final metaphor, the turn-and-turn-again quality of the words 'vegetable king', 'sprig', 'weed', 'beards', and 'hectoring' that guarantees there shall be no capitulation before the ideal of heroism.

A final point suggests itself. I have said that in stanza five it is not clear how far the poet is speaking of the 'thirties writers themselves and how far he is talking about the idea of heroism in the abstract; and I would add that the play on the word 'hectoring' in the last stanza keeps this ambiguity alive. I suspect that the poet deliberately fosters the ambiguity because by so doing he avoids any risk of getting away from the possible fact that the Macspaunday group was not remarkable for heroism. The quality of generalisation guards against historical inaccuracy. Yet it is always a very difficult matter to decide how far *fact* can impinge on a poem's *truth*. *Remembering the Thirties* appeals to fact, because unless we know something about the actual Macspaunday group we shall miss many of the poem's allusions and mimicries. But it is probably true to say that although these facts are of importance to a right understanding of the poem, the writer's estimation of them has to be justified inside the poem itself. And if this is so, we do not need to journey beyond the poem to decide whether the poet has been honest in his argument about the blending of the heroic and the absurd, nor do we need to know whether the Macspaunday group was in fact dedicated to heroism. Indeed, by widening the range of his two stanzas, the poet himself guards us from irrelevant fact-grubbing. As the title of his poem suggests, *Remembering the Thirties* is a personal statement derived from an actual historical moment, and we need to know no more about that moment than makes it possible for us to judge the adequacy of the poet's statement. In short, while the third stanza of part II *may* be indictable for inaccuracy, whether or not the Macspaunday group did or did not play the fool in order not to appear as fools is not of final importance to the poem; what is, is how the poet sets about convincing himself and us that the idea of heroism may involve an acceptance of the absurd.

Hornet and *Low Lands* are very different kinds of poems from *Remembering the Thirties*. At first they seem readily classifiable as nature poems. But a closer look suggests that they are not simply descriptive pieces. Both poems brood over the worlds they confront in a way that makes the brooding just as much the subject of the poems as the hornet and lowlands themselves. Both poems, I suggest, strive for the utmost open-mindedness and enlargement of the poet's sympathies. And here it is worth noting that both poems are markedly more free in metre and rhythm than the poem we have previously examined. They mingle iamb and anapaest without slavish regard for a metric norm and the number of syllables per line varies from ten to fourteen. This is not metrical licentiousness, it is proper flexibility in the interest of rendering the expressiveness of the poet's inner voice.

The subject of *Hornet* is a traditional one for an Englishman, who for centuries has admitted the fascination Italy has for him, in its alien southernness against his northernness. Yet having said this much I want immediately to add that we must avoid the risk of inflating the poem; we have instead to recognise its tact. For although *Hornet* is about the Englishman's sense of Italy's strange foreignness, even perhaps its 'otherness', it is so in a modest and scrupulously limited way.

The first stanza embodies a sense of brutal power that the poet senses in this strange land:

> . . . *what*
> *Must be a hornet volleys lethally back*
> *And forth in the air.*

How that word 'must' suggests a wonder beyond reassurance! And how the second enjambment enacts the lethal volleying as it

137

ricochets over the line ending. Such violence of movement finds its counterpart in the violence of colour contrast between the 'blindingly white Italian stone' and the 'blue-black' hornet. The diction itself gives force to the perception, with the explosive sound and stress on 'blue-black', and we may note how the syntax slams 'blue-black' against 'stone'.

By contrast, the second stanza is leisured in pace and syntax. The poet has returned to familiar ground and his musings are relaxed and at ease (even the rat-catcher is 'obligingly' bowed). But the third stanza swings back to the present and the strange; leisured reverie is displaced by the urgency of the

> *blue,*
> *Gun-metal blue, blue-black ominous ranger*
> *Of Italy's air.*

The repeated words act out a struggle towards refinement of perception, and they suggest the effort to grasp what cannot be 'known' in any contented way (as the wasp-coloured hornets of England can—and note how the word 'surely' of stanza two implies exactly the reassurance that 'gun-metal' and 'ominous' in the third stanza deny). Yet for all the sense of being adrift from certainties that the third stanza brings, the fourth and last is open-minded enough to yield an implicit confession of the excitement of the strange and the boredom of the familiar. It contrasts the England of 'pierced shadows'—the phrase suggests temperate heat, a blending of light and shade, a certain passiveness—with the extremes of Italy—violent, urgent, ceaselessly active. Note, for example, how 'strides' of line three pairs off against 'stains' of line four: England's energy is insidious, it defeats those oppositions of black and white which are so shockingly strange to English eyes and which, for all their ominousness, have a vitality, even exuberance, that the England of the poem does not have.

Hornet is a beautifully judged poem, because its implications are so many and yet its tactfully limited way of releasing those implications forbids us any large-scale comments. It is a meditation on and response to a small group of perceptions tested against knowledge the poet can bring to them. It probes for distinctions and contrasts in order to prise open the poet's capacity for responsiveness.

Low Lands does very much the same thing, except that in this case comparisons rather than contrasts are what matter. The first stanza makes clear just how metrically free this poem is. We are introduced to a voice—musing, absorbed, hesitant—that is given as much licence as is possible without the stanza falling into metrical chaos. The second line is a particularly masterful example of this fruitful tension between form and freedom; its basis is the iambic pentameter, but it has departed a long way from a rigid adherence to the norm. Indeed this line is in the great tradition of the plain style of English poetry and it typifies an important feature of *Low Lands*, for we are bound to recognise how little the verse form tries to impose on or in any way inhibit the experience the poet engages with and struggles to understand (with one significant exception, which I shall consider in a moment). The formal demands that the poem makes are just enough to ensure that the poet will give coherent articulation to his thoughts; but in no sense do they aim to impair the integrity of those thoughts. It is precisely the poet's ability to honour the demands of his form and of his subject that makes *Low Lands* such a masterly performance. And in the first stanza form and subject exist in a tension that helps to register an 'uncertain sense' of beauty. For the poet is struggling to define complex and 'uncertain' attitudes towards the low lands, what repels him, what attracts him.

The complexity is beautifully present in the second stanza. The image of the snake sets up an idea of treachery, something almost evilly unpleasant. Yet the stanza's cadences quite belie the idea. How lovingly the voice hovers over 'serpentine iridescence', how it lingers on the 'slow light spilt', how the enjambment of 'calm/Inundations' catches the very calmness the words describe as the voice unfolds the long word at the beginning of the line. If we concentrate on what the poet says in this stanza we note his irritation with and near-fear of the lowlands (no wonder he began by saying he could not live there, they threaten him). But if we concentrate on the *way* he says this, we understand something of the ingratitude he also admitted to in the first stanza, and why he has to confess to the low lands' uncertain beauty. And of course we need to concentrate on both aspects. For what the stanza explores is the poet's richly equivocal attitude to the lowlands.

But the third stanza is a different matter. For here, in the first three lines, regular iambics quite suddenly assume control and the diction exhibits a tendency towards what is surely self-conscious archaism. In addition, the details of the scene are 'literary', and altogether the stanza provides what is very nearly a pastiche of that old literary theme, of the fertility of harmonious nature. It is as though the poet consigns the low lands to the past, irritated by an almost rank luxuriance where even the rats can run sleek and lissom. And the last line, with its abrupt abandonment of the regular iambics, releases the poet's gathered irritation. We note the hint of venom in 'swells' and 'sac', the almost contemptuously brutal delivery of the last word, 'flat'.

In the next stanza we encounter another shift. Now the poet's attitude has become more relaxed, as though in deference to his recognition of the land's defencelessness against his attacks. And so this stanza, with its cluster of exclamation marks, its bizarre image revealing the ambiguity of the poet's attitude to a land which is like a defenceless person, calling out love, pity, condescension, irritation, complacence, and so on. Not that any one or two of these attitudes control; the point is rather that the stanza engages all of them, as the poet strives to find exactly what *is* the correct response to the land, what it is that will allow him to be most true to himself and it. And in the last stanza he stumbles on the truth.

> But a beauty there is, noble, dependent, unshrinking,
> In being at somebody's mercy, wide and alone.

The acknowledgement brings into the open what the first and second stanzas had hinted at and it makes clear exactly why his attitudes had fluctuated so widely in stanzas three and four. Here is the crucial discovery; that the nature of the land encourages all sorts of dramatising of the poet's relationship with it, just because it is easier for him to take up a stance than admit how completely he has to rely on his own ability to prise open the truth of his regard for the land. Its contented vulnerability makes heavy demands on the integrity of its judge, and it is this integrity that is illuminated in the last stanza.

Of course, to put it this way is to make the poem seem what it very obviously is not, a crudely moralistic tract. Yet we can hardly avoid recognising how the low lands provide the occasion for self-investigation and that they are of value to the poet because their very passivity forces him to look closely at the adequacy of his own attitudes to them. So the last lines fittingly suggest that any artist can benefit from living in a country which, far from providing for all his needs, is valuable precisely because it forces him to recognise the prime need—of self-honesty and consequently the mental enlargement that is necessary to the creation of worthwhile art.

It will be obvious that *Low Lands* is by no means an easy poem to write about. Indeed, I might say that the irreducible integrity of its manner makes almost inevitable a critic's oversimplifying or inflating or coarsening of the poem. Certainly I do not suppose that I have avoided these faults. Yet this is perhaps as it must be, and it is valuable in so far as our consciousness of our own inadequacies makes us strive constantly to refine our responses to a work of art and to find the words that will best do justice to them. For in the last analysis we have to hope that our intensely personal responses and findings are not at all subjective ones; and we can receive assurance that they are not by rendering those responses and findings as nearly as we can, so that other readers can check theirs against ours.

Other poems that provide a good introduction to Donald Davie are: *The Garden Party* and *Wood Pigeons at Raherny* (from *Brides of Reason*); *Time Passing* and *Under St Paul's* (from *A Winter Talent*); *Dedications* (1. *Wide France*; 2. *Barnsley Cricket Club*), *Housekeeping*, *A Christening*, *Bolyai*, *The Geometer* (all from *Events and Wisdoms*).

FRANK PRINCE
The Old Age of Michelangelo

Commentary by Michael Black

The Old Age of Michelangelo

Sometimes the light falls here too as at Florence
Circled by low hard hills, or in the quarry
Under its half-hewn cliffs, where that collection
Of pale rough blocks, still lying at all angles on the dust-white
    floor
Waits, like a town of tombs.

5   I finish nothing I begin.
And the dream sleeps in the stone, to be unveiled
Or half-unveiled, the lurking nakedness;
Luminous as a grapeskin, the cold marble mass
Of melted skeins, chains, veils and veins,

10 Bosses and hollows, muscular convexities,
Supple heroic surfaces, tense drums
And living knots and cords of love:
—Sleeps in the stone, and is unveiled
Or half-unveiled, the body's self a veil,

15 By the adze and the chisel, and the mind
Impelled by torment.
                    In the empty quarry
The light waits, and the tombs wait,
For the coming of a dream.

*   *   *

The power with which I imagine makes these things,
20 This prison:
And while the dream stirs in the stone, wakes in its chains,
Sometimes I think that I have spent my whole life making
    tombs,
And even those are unfinished. And yet, chafing,
Sadly closed there, in a rich bare case

25 Of bodily loveliness like solid sleep,
One sees the soul that turns
Waking, stretched on her side as if in pain, and how she sees
Browed like the dawn, the dark world
—Like a sulky pale cold louring dawn—

30 Loathing her hope of fruit, the pure bare flank:

144

Or else one sees her sunk in rest,
Letting her worn head droop over her empty body
And the much-pulled breasts hang dry,
Fallen, with long flat nipples.

35 And there is always
Some victor and some vanquished, always the fierce substance
And the divine idea, a drunkenness
Of high desire and thought, or a stern sadness:
And while it rests or broods or droops,
40 There will be always some great arm or shoulder
To incur or to impose some heavy torment,
There will be always the great self on guard, the giant
Reclined and ominous,
With back half-turned, hunched shoulder
45 And the enormous thigh
Drawn up as if disdainful,
Almost the bare buttock offered:
There will be always
A tall Victory with beaten Age
50 Doubled beneath its bent knee, but ignoring
(The naked proud youth bending aside
His vacuous burning brow and wide
Beautiful eyes and blank lips) but ignoring
The sad sordid slave, the old man.

*   *   *

55 And now I have grown old,
It is my own life, my long life I see
As a combat against nature that is our enemy
Holding the soul a prisoner by the heel;
And my whole anxious life I see
60 As a combat with myself, that I do violence to myself,
To bruise and beat and batter
And bring under
My own being,
Which is an infinite savage sea of love.

*   *   *

65 For you must know I am of all men ever born
Most inclined to love persons, and whenever I see someone
Who has gifts of mind and body, and can say or show me
     something
Better than the rest,
Straightway I am compelled
70 To fall in love with him, and then I give myself
Up to him so completely, I belong no longer to myself,
He wresting from me
So great part of my being, I am utterly
Bewildered and distraught, and for many days know nothing
75 Of what I am doing or where I am.
—Young green wood spits in burning,
Dry wood catches the flame: and I become now
An old man with a face like wrinkled leather, living alone,
And with no friends but servants,
80 Parasites, bad disciples puffed up by my favours, or else Popes,
Kings, cardinals or other patrons, being as for myself alone
Either a lord or subject, either with my gossips and buffoons
And clumsy fawning relatives; or towards you and such as
     you,
Whom I adore, an abject:

                    Messer THOMAS

85 CAVALIERE
I am naked in that sea of love
Which is an infinite savage glowing sea,
Where I must sink or swim. Cold, burning with sorrow,
I am naked in that sea and know
90 The sad foam of the restless flood
Which floats the soul or kills, and I have swum there
These fifty years and more,
And never have I burned and frozen
More than I have for you,
95 Messer Tommaso.

            *   *   *

Moon-cold or sun-hot, through what alternations
Of energy, long languor,

                    146

Periods of mad defiance, periods of fear, flight, misery
Cowering darkly,
100 Moon-cold or sun-hot, love that grips
Sun, moon, eternal hatred
Eternal hope and pain, packed close in one man's body,
And drawn, leaning to others.
                              And one other:
Grey eyes float in the dry light
105 That might draw Venus' car, moving at morning
Grey eyes through dry dark shadows, floating
Over the blocked ways, the despair,
And opening wide lids, irises
More starlike than the stars, purer than they, alive in the
        pale air,
110 Fire, life in thin dry air
Drawing the soul out at the mouth
Beauty in triumph,
My defeat.

              *   *   *

—I am always alone, I speak to no one
115 But that shabby Bernardo, nor do I wish to:
Trudging up and down Italy, wearing out my shoes and life,
Toiling still to grow poorer, ugly, sad,
Proud, narrow, full of unfulfilled desires!

Yet I have come to Rome, rich in its ruins, and for the last time,
120 As if I made to cross a little stream dry-foot
That had divided us, and yet again, for the last time
My dream grows drunk within me,
And opens its great wings and like an eagle
Wild naked perfect pure, soars from its nest.
125 Almost I am persuaded, almost, that it is possible,
My love, like anybody's love, is possible.
My eye stares on your face, and my old mind
Soars naked from its cliff, and thinks to find
—Drunk with illumination as the sky itself is drunken
130 Or a dry river-bed with light—
The wild path to its thought, for all is passion

Here, even cogitation, and it climbs and clambers, floats and
     flings
And hovers, it is thrust up, it is hurled
Throbbing into the stillness,
135 Rapt, carried by the blissful air
Borne up, rebuffs and buffets
—Having hurled
The dead world far below it—
Stretches out long rapturous claws and wings,
140 Stiff as with agony, shakes as with tenderness
And dives and hovers at you, swoops and aches
To stun, caress
And beat you to your knees,
Clutches and clings,

145 —As if it would grow one with you and carry
Up the solitary sky
That strange new beautiful identity,
Where it might never fade or melt or die!
And many things
150 Are put about and taken up and spread abroad
About Michelangelo, poor old man, but when I
Come to you, I care nothing
For honour or the world, I only care
To look long on your face, and let
155 The dream soar from its nest. For do I know
Myself, what I should mean? I only know
That if I had those wings, not in a dream,
And I could open, beat those wings;
If I could clutch you in the claws of dream,
160 And take you up with me in loneliness
To the roof-tree, angle of heaven, vault
Of exquisite pale buffeted glare:
I should gain or regain
The heaven of that high passion, pallor, innocence
165 —I should gain or regain
The sole pure love, and fence it with my wings.

*   *   *

But my two eyes
Are empty, having wept, and my skin stretched
Like an old hide over dry bones, and my face
170 *Grown flat and timorous, broken,*
Loving or having loved this dream.
And the light fades from the sky, the dream dies in the stone
Slowly, I finish nothing I begin, and in my evening
Last torments and last light, torn hesitations
175 *Between desire and fear, between desire and my disdain*
—Emerging into dusky rooms, high halls, rich architecture
And the tawny roofs of Rome. For this love discovers only
The world's desert and death, the dusty prison
Where we have shut ourselves, or the sky shuts us.

180 *Fades the light, and below there*
I lie, an old man like a fallen god propped up:
My eyes close, and my head hangs,
Heavy as if with love-drink or with dreams,
And from my old thick swagging side
185 *Pours forth a marble river. Overhead floats*

A face, two brilliant eyes
That make the whole world pale,
Floating, and that great nobleness,
That great despising, of the mind
190 *To which the beautiful is as the felt heat*
Of the fire of the eternal.

Do not forget the poor old man.

NOTE: On the poet's authority line 176 has been corrected: 'halls' being preferred to the former reading 'walls'.

The poem opens quietly, in a meditative tone. The word 'light' (1)* proves to be thematic: one of the recurring preoccupations which gives the poem its structure. The old sculptor, now living in Rome, is reminded, by a trick of the light, of his early life in Florence. There is a shift of vision: he sees Florence itself in his mind's eye, and the quarry where he worked. 'Low hard' (2) darkens the

* Numbers in brackets are line numbers.

tonality, implies oppression or obstruction; 'half-hewn' (3) hints at incompletion and frustrated effort. Then the 'pale rough blocks' (4), at first disorderly in a long undisciplined sentence (resistant to the ordering mind of the artist?), fall into a pattern, but a dismaying one: for he sees 'a town of tombs' (5). The accent falls here, painfully, and the movement is checked for a moment.

The mind takes up again, after this heavy caesura, but in order to reflect sadly on its failures: 'I finish nothing I begin'. The still slow, hesitant, sombre movement begins to quicken at the apprehension of its own distress. Another theme, 'the dream' (6), is brought in by a natural counter-association: tombs, deaths, failures, remind him of what he had wanted to bring to *life*: 'the dream sleeps in the stone'. The tone brightens as he imagines what the achievement would have been: to have 'unveiled' (third theme) or—and for a moment it seems equally satisfying—to have left 'half-unveiled', the 'lurking nakedness' in the block (6–7). And now that nakedness comes into the light, a sculptor's light, and wonderful lines follow (8–12) where the surfaces glow and are transparent, are felt, seem to plunge and swell like sinew and muscle under skin, are created in word and rhythm as he had sought to realise them in stone, with a lover's hand. Indeed he comes up against the word 'love' (12), and it is painful, for the 'knots and cords of love' also belong to bonds and whips. He is checked again, and returns to his sense of failure: all this 'sleeps in the stone'; when he completes a statue he has 'unveiled' something; when he cannot finish, it is 'half-unveiled'. But to strip off the stone to the naked statue, to take the clothes off a naked body, is in any case only to half-unveil, for the body itself is a veil (14). So his failures, his incompletions, may be emblematic of a deep fear that what he is attempting *cannot* succeed: there is a final knowledge one cannot reach. Hence the 'torment' (16) of the mind—another painful pause. The first movement of the poem ends quietly and sadly, with a return to the now 'empty' quarry (exhausted of its stone? recognised as delusive?), the light, the tombs—a sheaf of themes—all waiting. And now the main theme is reintroduced: they are waiting for 'the coming of a dream' (18). The movement ends.

There has been a momentary fire, an access of energy, which has died down. Now the mind resumes, discursively, conceptually, but with a touch of pride. The 'torment' of 16 is turned into 'the power with which I imagine' (19). Are 'these things' the sculptures or his present imaginings, or both? The depressive reaction follows the momentary sense of power in three contrastive syllables: 'This prison' (20). So the same 'power' reveals his captivity and the bondage in which his creations lie. Positive and negative movements lie parallel in the next two lines as well. He imagines 'the dream' stirring, waking 'in its chains' (21) as he works on a statue, yet at the same time, reflecting on actual commissions, he remembers with irony how much time he has spent on literal tombs (22)—'And even those are unfinished' (23). The mind begins to warm and quicken again, for the train of thought has brought back to mind—to concrete sensual apprehension—one of these tombs, on which he had represented an aspect of the dream. It showed the 'soul' (another theme) (26),

> Sadly closed there, in a rich bare case
> Of bodily loveliness like solid sleep; (24–5)

—two crucial lines of great solidity. The soul is sad at its imprisonment ('closed . . . in a case') in the body; and yet the naked body does provide a 'rich bare case' of 'loveliness'. Is the body a tomb, a death? This is a darkening of the thought about the body as a veil (14): it is something the soul has to be liberated from. The embodied soul turns, waking; but this is painful (27)—like a birth or a death perhaps, and this symbolises his whole effort, his whole thought. 'Browed like the dawn' is 'her' attribute, not that of 'the dark world' in 28. This—another figure to which she turns in the dawn as to a lover—proves a threat to her, envious of her virginity which is also 'hope of fruit' (30). Because 'she' is awakening, has a 'bodily loveliness' which is like 'solid sleep' she—the soul—is associated with the dream, which is also a dawn. It is already beginning to seem a little like a delusion: the feeling is reinforced when a third figure (31–4) comes into view, female like the first, but its converse: not virginal but worn with child-bearing and now barren, not dawn but evening. If the first was like a hope of birth or creation, this one might be the sculptor's sense of exhaustion, dried-upness, and frustrated effort. All this is conveyed in a direct physical evocation, which goes beyond the statues themselves to what they body forth.

The thought moves on, again working through a physical embodiment of its preoccupations. The mind presents to itself other polar opposites and struggles that condition its existence: the conflict between 'substance' and 'idea' (36–7), the 'drunkenness' (another theme), or equally the 'stern sadness' of 'high desire and thought': a sense of the ecstasy of an idealism, qualified by knowledge of the ascetic discipline needed to pursue it, and darkened by the thought that it may be a delusion. And while 'it' (39)—and this is a continuation of the feeling about the representatives of the soul, the female figures in the previous paragraph—'rests or broods or droops' (39) (he thinks of it as a characteristically static figure, gathered or relaxed) there is opposed to it—and another sculpture comes into focus—the opposite principle, dangerous, uncomprehending, scornful and violent (40–7): an evocation of a menacing male figure, muscular, brutal, and identified with 'the great self on guard' (42). It is perhaps a conscious daylight mind, a male will, dominating and contemptuous; it both 'incurs' and 'imposes' 'heavy torment' (41)—on the aspiration associated with the female figures, one wonders? Then, harking back to 'some victor and some vanquished' (36), he turns to another image, another emblem-sculpture. 'There will be always' (48) also an emblematic victory in which 'The sad sordid slave, the old man' (another theme: it is himself he means) is conquered and scorned by a naked proud youth (51). The feeling towards the youth is complicated: he arouses sexual feelings, but his 'burning brow' is 'vacuous', his lips 'blank'. It is his eyes—a further theme—which are 'beautiful' (53).

That movement ends with the words 'the old man' at the end of a vigorous and plastic evocation. He is brought back to himself after that vain movement outwards, that second gesture of effort towards the creative ideal realm, the effort to seize in words what he has been trying to present through his sculpture: to sum up his internal life of aspiration. He is back with himself in a humiliating aspect: the figure of the slave conveys his age, his defeat, his sadness, and in 'sordid' a hint of self-hate, or of fear of his reflection in the eyes of those he loves.

The next paragraph picks up the word 'old' (54, 55), and directly contemplates his present life. He begins to make sense of, by turning into concepts, those sculptured images of aspiration, alternation, conflict, contempt, and failure that have recurred to his mind. His life has been a combat against the conditions of existence, against his humanness (seen as a limiting thing), and against himself (56-8). 'Nature that is our enemy' (57) was perhaps glimpsed in the 'great self' (42); it is the life and death of the body, which holds the soul (cf. 26) a prisoner (58, but the word harks back to the prison in line 20, the chains of 9 and 21). Again he sways into sensual evocation in the rhythm of

> bruise and beat and batter
> And bring under . . . (61-2)

This is the sculptor's activity, but seen also as an effort at beating his way out of prison, at self-mortification, as boxing with an opponent who turns out to be himself (the great pugilist figure incurring or imposing heavy torment in 41). 'Bring under' implies a victory (49-54) which is a creative struggle, but also a personal one, for what he has to defeat is also

> My own being,
> Which is an infinite savage sea of love (64).

And this capacity has been hinted at, in its saddest aspect, in 49-54. And 'bruise and beat and batter' reminds us of the 'knots and cords of love' (12). Slaves are beaten (54).

There follows a straightforward passage (65-75) of direct tatement about his capacity for love, of excellence as well as beauty. For a moment it moves into metaphor: 'young green wood spits in burning' (76) suggests the young man's resistance to his own desire; 'dry wood catches the flame' suggests his own painful susceptibility in old age, but also the purity and intensity of his flame. ('Dryness' is a recurring theme.) He contemplates his ugliness, his loneliness, the inadequacy of such relationships as he has (77-83), their alternation between disdain and abjectness. Then he veers, helplessly, into a passionate declaration. The rather plain, direct, reasonable passage from 65 onwards has been a preparation, a foil, for this outburst. He moves from the fawning relatives, and the thought of his abjectness 'towards you and such as you' (83) (a rather bitter little phrase) 'whom I adore'. The caesura shows him taking breath; the uttering of the name 'Messer THOMAS/CAVALIERE' is like a dedication, or an address on a letter, or just a cry. Line 64 had introduced the figure of the sea, but he had turned away into rationalisation. Now he is *in* the sea, and calling from it. He is naked in it; he says so twice (86 and 89): it is the condition of a lover, a statue, as well as a bather—perhaps a drowned man. The 'savage glowing sea' (87) in which he is both cold because alone and comfortless (unloved?) and burning with desire and sorrow (88) shows that love is a tormenting element, a region of purgatory—a reminiscence of Dante, perhaps. Its foam is 'sad'; it is 'restless'. The central fact about it is that it 'floats' the soul: it sustains, or liberates, or kills. The soul is the prisoner of the body, we know from lines 14, 25, 58. Love is its proving ground, the means by which we transcend limitations, in a kind of triumph which is also like a death. We have to give ourselves to that sea. And now he has found his greatest love (91–4). The plaintiveness of 93–5, the abjectness almost, hint that he suspects it may be a vain love: he is playing 'sad sordid slave' to a 'tall Victory'.

Lines 96–113, the next movement, are entirely metaphorical, starting in a mode which reminds me of some of Eliot's poetry.* The see-sawing alternatives of the first lines are an evocation, as in a delirium, of his anguished states of love. The 'eternal hope and pain' is his side of the exchange. He thinks of this as a magnetic attraction, or the pull of gravity towards 'others'. But he goes on: beyond the mere 'others' there is *one* ideal other (103). There 'floats' before him a vision of 'grey eyes' which have total power and significance. They move through the 'dry dark shadows' signifying illumination and refreshment; they 'float' (again, and cf. 91) over blocked ways, leading him out of impasses and frustrations. The movement becomes elated and triumphant, the imagery ethereal and ecstatic (108–12). These eyes (the beautiful eyes in 53 had been

* I am reminded of *Ash Wednesday* by the antiphonal rhythms. Mr T. R. Barnes points out that 'Moon-cold or sun-hot' (96) may be an unconscious reminiscence of 'Mooncold or moonhot' in *Rannoch, by Glencoe*, the fourth of the 'Landscapes'.

an earthly embodiment of this beauty) have power magnetically to draw the soul, the essence, towards the centre of life and creation, out of the mouth—as in a mystical union, or death. It is 'beauty in triumph' (112). At once he falls from the high point: the negative movement follows: 'My defeat.' The two words compress the thoughts that in these living relationships the other is the victor, and that his art, being founded on the physical, cannot directly represent what he wants to convey, which is to do with the spirit. He is back in the world as he knows it to be, with the self-confessed paradox of his art.

The next movement begins with a few lines (114–18) which lead on from his sense of defeat. He contemplates, perhaps self-pityingly exaggerating, his shabbiness, his ugliness, his loneliness. He makes himself almost ridiculous. But in the line

Proud, narrow, full of unfulfilled desires! (118)

he begins to erect himself again: the line itself is obstinately proud. And he starts a new effort upwards. Lines 119–24 are longer, with a strong recurring pulse. He is making himself a base from which to take off into a great soaring movement, an ecstasy longer sustained (130–66). Line 119 sets off, as it were, firmly: 'for the last time' suggests determination, nearing home. Line 120 makes light of intervening obstacles. 'For the last time' sounds again, excitedly (121), for as he says 'My dream' (the long-awaited dream? one wonders) 'grows drunk within me' (122). 'Drunk' suggests an intelligent reservation, as well as the ecstasy. His dream becomes a winged creature, with powerful mythical associations. The strong rhythm, opening out like the wings, begins to soar (124). What had been naked in the sea in his agony is now naked in the air in his triumph. Has he died as a body in the sea, to be taken into the air as a soul? Lines 125–6 enact his excitement, but the two 'almosts' convey his remaining reservations. That his love might be 'possible' goes beyond the homosexuality, the difference of age, to the essential requirement. Through the body it would approach the spirit; but it would be 'possible' only if answered by an equivalent movement of the spirit. Again he imagines himself rapt in contemplation of the beloved; and his 'old mind/Soars naked from its cliff' (127-8). To fall into the infinite savage sea and drown, like Icarus? Or like Daedalus to fly? Or like Jove to seize Ganymede?

Lines 131-44 create, with the driving cross-rhythms of Hopkins, the feel of successfully riding the air: from 139-44 he is Jove the eagle, swooping on the youth. But below this intoxication the undermining intelligence and self-knowledge are at work. 'Drunk' and 'drunken' recur in 129. 'Drunk with illumination' is a densely packed summary of his condition: the 'illumination' is both spiritual enlightenment and the blinding reflection of light in the parched mountain water-course up which he imagines himself stumbling: the 'wild path' to the summit of his thought, to which he 'climbs and clambers' and then 'floats' from. The image of the dry river-bed which is the polar opposite implied by the image of drunkenness fuses three themes: light, dryness, drunkenness (129-30), and reflects back on his age, his exhaustion, his barrenness, his self-deception. The stony river-bed dissolves into the path of the air (131), an unsure footing. The imagined mastery of the air is partly a matter of rejecting the 'dead world' (reality); and in the blissful air he finds himself giving rebuffs and buffets (136). There is something desperate in the whole effort: an attempt to convince the self against the grain of the intelligence, indeed a link backwards with the boxing match with the 'great self'. Characteristically, and horribly, having become the eagle, he stretches predatory claws at the youth (139), wants to 'beat you to your knees', thus reversing the humiliation of 49-54. 'Clutches and clings' (144) hints at the violence of dependence.

There is indeed a pause here, a change of rhythm, but the dream *will* be indulged, and carries on unchecked for four more lines (145-8). The two are to go up into some heaven, forming 'a strange new beautiful identity' which would in that unheard-of place 'never fade or melt or die'. 'Melt' might be a reference to Icarus, an ironic comment.

For a moment he checks himself, remembering that he is in the world, and gossiped about (149-51). He puts on his rather repulsive deprecating self-pity ('poor old man'). He dismisses the thought, and reverts to the soaring dream (155). But he is flogging it into the air: it is a pathetic and desperate as well as a noble illusion. He begins to repeat the word 'dream' (155, 157, 159) and it begins to look more and more like self-deception. He admits a moment of confusion (156) but turns doggedly back. If it were *not* in a dream (157)—a sad concession—if he could 'clutch' the beloved in 'the claws of dream' (159, the predatory note again), he would take him 'in loneliness' to the 'roof-tree, angle of heaven'. This is a 'vault of exquisite pale buffetted glare': diffuse light, contending wind, dazzled vision (162). Here he would gain or regain 'high passion, pallor, innocence' (which sound very limited values to me, and somewhat *fin de siècle*, but we are being asked to place them): he would regain the 'sole pure love, and fence it with my wings' (166). Again the note of defensive possessiveness.

He falls completely out of this imagined heaven. Line 167 brings back the theme of emptiness and dryness, associated with age (cf. 33, 104, 106, where the eyes seemed to conquer drought; 114 where he imagined the eyes as life in thin dry air; the dry river bed of 130). Long sorrows have drained him; he is a dried carcase in a desert (169); he is disfeatured like a boxer. 'Having loved this dream' (171) sounds, because of the past tense, like a renunciation, a recognition of his delusion, as well as a renunciation of the creative power given him by the dream. The themes crowd in, all in the minor. The 'light fades' (172) where it had 'waited' in 17; the 'dream dies in the stone' where in 6 it had slept in the stone. Again he finishes nothing he begins (173, 5). His evening is last torments (174, 16) and 'last light'. His surroundings reestablish themselves around him as reality (176-7). He makes his bleak summating statement

> For this love discovers only
> The world's desert and death,

(Rome, which has swum back into focus, is emblematic of the world's nothingness)

> the dusty prison
> Where we have shut ourselves, or the sky shuts us. (179)

Rome, the dusty enclosing prison, is the world; but also the body; perhaps too the final metamorphosis of the 'low hard hills' round Florence (2) or the quarry circled by its cliffs where the pale blocks (anxious for life?) waited, sometimes vainly, to be resurrected into the eternal life of art. In that release, that revelation of an immortality of a kind, the artist had tried to find the type of another release: the inwardness of the soul behind the veil of the body. And a third release too: the union in love, to create a more perfect identity (147). All this was delusion: the failure in love reflects despair on all his aspirations, for it is his kind of integrity not to separate one realm from another. When he had been unable to finish what he had begun (5,173), his leaving the figure partly imprisoned in the block is an admission of the other failures. The prison, the chains, the blocked ways, the dried-up riverbed are the condition of life.

The rest is postlude, and yet a transforming one. The thematic light continues to fade (180). He imagines himself in this dusk like an antique river god, a contrast with the reclining female figures which symbolised the soul in 23–30. He is falling asleep, or dying (is the river-god also a dying gladiator figure?). 'Heavy as if with love-drink or with dreams' (183) is a final comment on his 'drunkenness', his ecstasy. The 'heaviness' of the 'drink' generates the idea that like the river god, like the gladiator, he does indeed give forth, but he can only bleed a 'marble river' (185): a summary of his spiritual drought, a link with the dried-up river-bed, and a suggestion that his sculptures are his true creation, his children. 'My old thick swagging side' is a fine Shakespearean concretion: conveying congelation and physical coarseness as well as the heavy curve of the propped-up body. 'Pours forth' (at last! after so much drought) is an irony; but it in turn generates 'floats' in the same line. Such is the persistence of the spirit's desires that he still sees, even as he renounces, the mirage of the supremely beautiful eyes, which devalue the world of reality. He sees too what, positively, they stand for. The repeated 'floating' as in 91, 104, 106, is affirmative; the element is lived in and conquered, the desert is irrigated, the marble river transformed. He can still point towards the 'great nobleness', the 'great despising' of the mind. The alternation between disdain and abjectness which had exasperated him is now resolved. He can also, in his darkness, point to a lifelong aspiration; his was a mind

To which the beautiful is as the felt heat
Of the fire of the eternal. (191)

So the dominant image of the poem, light, is referred to its source, the emblematic sun, and to something transcendent beyond. This is the central power of the universe, illuminating bodily beauty and the beauty of art. It fosters them both. Beauty is its showing forth, its 'felt heat', a source of life and comfort.

The poem has quietly turned itself, after all that struggle, into an affirmation in spite of the defeat. The last line

> *Do not forget the poor old man.*

comes from the artist who has in his work left us intimations which ensure that we do not forget him. The words are spoken quietly, with acceptance and a kind of confidence.

Such a paraphrase, inevitably laborious and dry, can at any rate be offered without any misgiving that it could be taken as a substitute for the original. Prince's poem is perhaps 'difficult'; it is certainly long and complex and its structure has to be sought in its themes and figures. But it has passages of such magnificent directness and vigour (for instance, lines 5–16; 23–34; 39–47: all the passages where the sculpture is evoked; and the whole enactment of the ecstatic dream and the awakening from it—119–66) that the reader is instantly seized with the way in which the 'thought' is 'felt'. I have merely plodded after, conceptualising.

And that is one interest, one quality of the poem. The things which the discursive intelligence separates or unravels and presents as concepts—ambitions, ideals, passions, talents, aspirations—are here presented as they might be experienced. They are gestures or impulsions of the whole mind moving together, all its 'departments' inextricably complicated. This is what it feels like both 'to have an idea' and to feel passionately about one's life: the two things are not of such different orders as we think. This is what it might be like to attempt to live by ideas: not as abstractions, but as things which one constructs, mingled (how could they not be?) with personal compulsions.

The grandeur of the poem for me is the imagination and the power with which this mind is projected. This is credibly a great mind, a powerful personality and a man of genius, imagined by a pure act of dramatic art, presented with his failings (if that is what they are): the self-pity, the mixture of misanthropy, pride, scorn, and pitiful dependence. Paradoxically, its success greatly mitigates the sadness of the poem. One feels the loneliness of the central figure as his greatest grief, and one is about to offer the cliché about the isolation of the human situation, and the double isolation of the great artist, when one reflects that Prince, by imagining that isolation and so convincingly conveying it, has greatly qualified it.

It is a possible Michelangelo, indeed a likely one. The achievement justifies itself, and it also has the representative interest I have just suggested. When one thinks also what Prince has avoided, one's respect grows. He has not, for instance, used the persona he has created as a puppet to think his own thoughts. He has not used him to make flat ironic contrasts between the glories of Renaissance Rome and the tawdriness of the present day. He has not fallen into W. H. Auden's easy, 'wry' *Musée des Beaux Arts* manner ('About suffering they were never wrong, The Old Masters'). The poem is properly serious and springs from a disinterested extension outwards of the mind. Since it has avoided these 'manners', one can note as a fact, rather than as a criticism, that some passages remind one of Hopkins, others of Eliot. That is only to say that these writers lend technical help. The Hopkins-like passages use one of his principal gifts—a movement which involves the reader physically in what it describes, so that it does not 'say', it 'does'. The influence of Eliot is related, less direct, but more pervasive: it is the gift of conveying 'thought' by non-conceptual means, what I. A. Richards called 'a music of ideas'. Although at the time of writing this poem Prince was specifically trying to avoid Yeats's manner, perhaps there is still a debt to Yeats: the gift of wholehearted utterance without inhibiting self-irony. There is a difference, of course: one cannot imagine Yeats so entirely immersed in another personality.

Two precursors are outstripped: the poets whom one might think of as forerunners in the genre of dramatic monologue by Renaissance figures—Browning and the early Ezra Pound. Prince gets far beyond Browning, who never rises above the interesting *fait divers* and a limited taste for 'psychology' (compare, for instance, *Pictor Ignotus*, *Fra Lippo Lippi*, and *Andrea del Sarto* in *Men and Women*). Pound would be shown up badly in any direct comparison between similar poems. He is too strikingly like Browning, for one thing (and like Maurice Hewlett, too). There is a great difference between kinds of self-projection. It is himself which Pound projects, as semi-learned hearty (see *Piere Vidal Old* in *Personae*); Prince has entirely suppressed himself in the effort to imagine the other person. On the other hand Professor Prince tells me that he is conscious of a debt to Pound: indeed the debt to Eliot and that to Pound are inextricable, since it was Pound who taught Eliot so many technical lessons. The austerity and delicacy of Pound's syntax and rhythms; the *procédé* of the later poems: these are influences.

I have worked on the conventional principle that the poem contains within itself the reasons why it is so and not otherwise. It is important to do this, simply so as to let the poem work. At certain moments, people who know Michelangelo's sculpture, architecture and writings are likely to recognise a familiar shape or phrase. But it is important, from lines 21 to 47, for instance, not to say simply 'Ah yes, the figures in the Medici chapel,' or at line 49, 'Ah yes, the Victory in the Palazzo Vecchio'. Messer Thomas Cavaliere existed; perhaps whole phrases in the poem come from the letters and poems. But I am partly led to say this because there are one or two passages which do not have the life and complexity of the rest of the poem; and one wonders whether a quotation or paraphrase has been taken into the structure without being fully assimilated. In any case, the poem works without these identifications, which are interesting but secondary. Prince is not painting word-pictures of the statues: he evokes them to indicate what they represent for his Michelangelo. These are the images in which his aspirations and torments were bodied forth.

It might be more interesting and useful (though it is still tangential to the poem) to relate the 'thought' to what one knows of Neoplatonism, Renaissance artistic theory and the other topics which one learns about in books on 'background'. One great point of the poem is that this schematic learning becomes dramatic. One comes to see Neoplatonism as something intrinsically tragic if the effort is made to live by it: the quaint terminology and outdated concepts do not themselves appear; instead they are turned into something on which a mind might indeed be painfully stretched. This is what it is like to have ideas made part of a mind, being taken into it and being lived. So the language is modern (compare Pound's affected archaism) and the feeling also seems modern, for that is the only way in which the ideas could be treated seriously. The whole notion of an 'influence' is transformed: perhaps the poet-dramatist is the only true historian of ideas?

The fragments of information are taken into the structure and used, released from their original context into the new one and made real. It may well be that particular sculptures, especially Michelangelo's habit of leaving them unfinished, and the writings, or some feeling about them, were the *données* from which the poem took off: particularly, perhaps, the feeling that the Medici chapel figures directly present emblems of the soul, expecially Dawn turning towards the light, which is also thought of as a lover in her dream. This recumbent figure is a type of many of Michelangelo's propped-up recumbent figures turning towards the spectator: at the end of the poem it has been transformed into the river-god, which is a type of fertility, and the gladiator, who is death. But what we have is not description, but the result of asking what sort of mind produced these things, in an effort towards what?

The poem is to be found in *The Doors of Stone* (1963), Prince's own selection from his poetry to that date. His long dramatic meditations seem to me to show his greatest power, though readers should test this statement for themselves. In the same book will also be found *An epistle to a patron* and *Strafford* the first a *tour de force* in the major key, the second (more complex, but I think less assured) in the minor.

ROBERT LOWELL
Waking Early Sunday Morning

Commentary by Edward Lucie-Smith

Waking Early Sunday Morning

O to break loose, like the chinook
salmon jumping and falling back,
nosing up to the impossible
stone and bone-crushing waterfall—
5   raw-jawed, weak-fleshed there, stopped by ten
steps of the roaring ladder, and then
to clear the top on the last try,
alive enough to spawn and die.

Stop, back off. The salmon breaks
10   water, and now my body wakes
to feel the unpolluted joy
and criminal leisure of a boy—
no rainbow smashing a dry fly
in the white run is free as I,
15   here squatting like a dragon on
time's heard before the day's begun!

Vermin run for their unstopped holes;
in some dark nook a fieldmouse rolls
a marble, hours on end, then stops;
20   the termite in the woodwork sleeps—
listen, the creatures of the night
obsessive, casual, sure of foot,
go on grinding, while the sun's
daily remorseful blackout dawns.

25   Fierce, fireless mind, running downhill.
Look up and see the harbour fill:
business as usual in eclipse
goes down to the sea in ships—
wake of refuse, dacron rope,
30   bound for Bermuda or Good Hope,
all bright before the morning watch
the wine-dark hulls of yawl and ketch.

I watch a glass of water wet
with a fine fuzz of icy sweat,

35   *silvery colors touched with sky,*
serene in their neutrality—
yet if I shift, or change my mood,
I see some object made of wood,
background behind it of brown grain,
40   *to darken it, but not to stain.*

O that the spirit could remain
tinged but untarnished by its strain!
Better dressed and stacking birch,
or lost with the Faithful at Church—
45   *anywhere, but somewhere else!*
And now the new electric bells,
clearly chiming, 'Faith of our fathers,'
and now the congregation gathers.

O Bible chopped and crucified
50   *in hymns we hear but do not read,*
none of the milder subtleties
of grace or art will sweeten these
stiff quatrains shovelled out four-square—
they sing of peace, and preach despair;
55   *yet they gave darkness some control,*
and left a loophole for the soul.

No, put old clothes on, and explore
the corners of the woodshed for
its dregs and dreck: tools with no handle,
60   *ten candle-ends not worth a candle,*
old lumber banished from the Temple,
damned by Paul's precept and example,
cast from the kingdom, banned in Israel,
the wordless sign, the tinkling cymbal.

65   *When will we see Him face to face?*
Each day, He shines through darker glass.
In this small town where everything
is known, I see His vanishing
emblems, His white spire and flag—

70   pole sticking out above the fog,
like old white china doorknobs, sad,
slight, useless things to calm the mad.

Hammering military splendor,
top-heavy Goliath in full armor—
75   little redemption in the mass
liquidation of their brass,
elephant and phalanx moving
with the times and still improving,
when that kingdom hit the crash:
80   a million foreskins stacked like trash . . .

Sing softer! But what if a new
diminuendo brings no true
tenderness, only restlessness,
excess, the hunger for success,
85   sanity of self-deception
fixed and kicked by reckless caution,
while we listen to the bells—
anywhere, but somewhere else!

O to break loose. All life's grandeur
90   is something with a girl in summer . . .
elated as the President
girdled by his establishment
this Sunday morning, free to chaff
his own thoughts with his bear-cuffed staff,
95   swimming nude, unbuttoned, sick
of his ghost-written rhetoric!

No weekends for the gods now. Wars
flicker, earth licks its open sores,
fresh breakage, fresh promotions, chance
100   assassinations, no advance.
Only man thinning out his kind
sounds through the Sabbath noon, the blind
swipe of the pruner and his knife
busy about the tree of life . . .

105   *Pity the planet, all joy gone*
      from this sweet volcanic cone;
      peace to our children when they fall
      in small war on the heels of small
      war—until the end of time
110   *to police the earth, a ghost*
      orbiting forever lost
      in our monotonous sublime.

Waking Early Sunday Morning is a poem which belongs to a very particular kind of modernist tradition—that of the attempt to come to terms with the events and feelings of the present by adapting the literary devices of the past, and then using these as a kind of persona—a mask through which the poet speaks, something held a little apart from his own personality. The form of the poem calls attention to this. The stanza-pattern is the same as the one which Marvell uses in *The Garden*, and *Upon Appleton House*, and there are other stylistic devices—such as the frequent use of paradox—which encourage us to read this as a work which is 'metaphysical' in the seventeenth-century sense. Lowell has previously stated of his earlier book *Life Studies* that he avoided strict metre because 'with that form it's hard not to have echoes of Marvell'. Here the identity of form seems to make it clear that the echoes are deliberate.

But of course Lowell remains a twentieth-century writer, and the strategies of his poem are necessarily different from those which Marvell might have adopted, had he felt moved to write on the same subject. *Waking Early Sunday Morning* is a meditation, despite the formality of the technique, and Lowell allows himself the freest possible play of association. Indeed, the poem moves forward by means of this, and such a progression would have been impossible to a writer of an earlier, pre-Freudian epoch.

The basic situation is very simple. The poet pictures himself rising out of sleep, and shares with us the thoughts which drift into his consciousness as he wakes. External events, such as the sound of the new electric church bells in stanza 6, or even the sight of a glass of water on a bedside table, are interwoven with the poet's thoughts and preoccupations. Wherever Lowell wants to depart a little from the 'natural' order of events, or the natural line of argument, he is able to refer us to the situation he has created. We all know that as we wake our thoughts only slowly organise themselves. The poem mimes this process of self-organisation—but only up to a certain point. The formality already mentioned, buttressed occasionally by some rather archaic turns of phrase ('Sing softer!' in line 81, for instance) serve to remind us that this is a carefully considered, highly wrought work of art.

The opening of the poem is one of the most cunningly calculated things about it. Lowell starts with an image which he means to use again at different point in the development, rather as a musician first states the theme of his composition. 'O to break loose,' he says, like the salmon going up river to spawn. The last line of the stanza brings us to the first of the paradoxes in which the poem abounds. The poet wants to be 'alive enough to spawn and die'. Death and fertility are deliberately placed in conjunction.

With the second verse, the poet checks himself. The image modulates. The salmon breaking water becomes identified with the act of waking itself, emergence into consciousness. We are immediately presented with another paradox—'unpolluted joy' is also 'the criminal leisure of a boy'—the happy child remains a being sunk in original sin. The writer declares that he is freer, even, than the glittering fish, but we notice that the fish is just about to be hooked ('smashing a dry fly'). This curious undermining of apparently forthright imagery continues throughout the third stanza as well as the second, until at last we are provided with an explanation. The use of the adjective 'unstopped', for example, suggests that some holes have been, or later will be, stopped, leaving the creatures of the night in the open and unprotected. A little later, the idea that 'the creatures of the night/go on grinding'—they labour in some way, or grind their daily bread—is set against the adjective 'casual'. The explanation comes with another epithet—'remorseful'—in line 24. The sun, dawning, imposes a kind of curfew on the nocturnal creatures, but it is the writer himself who feels remorse, danger and oppression, and hence the reversal, the use of the opposite word to the one we expect.

But again Lowell checks himself. Line 25 is a sudden gesture of self-reproach. The poet commands himself to look outside the window, and to observe the morning world beginning to go about its usual business, where modern technology—'dacron'—combines with all the weight of tradition—the Homeric epithet 'wine-dark'.

However, once the idea of 'looking' has entered his mind, the poet starts to concentrate his attention on what is probably the simplest object in his own immediate context, the glass of water on his bedside table, with its bloom of condensation. We are all aware that when the mind is, so to speak, 'idling', not yet in gear (and being slightly drunk or slightly sleepy are the likeliest moments) such simple objects can take on universal significance. We begin to experiment with our own perceptions—for instance, with the fact that the water in a glass is tinged or stained by what we see through its transparency, and yet itself remains pure. The succeeding verse immediately turns this notion into a comparison, and then intro-duces another experience—the sound of church-bells ringing. The poet feels that his thoughts are doing him no good—he should be 'anywhere but here'. Yet 'the Faithful at Church' are 'lost' we notice, and not saved.

With the six stanzas so far discussed, *Waking Early Sunday Morning* completes the first part of its trajectory. It is time for a second theme to be introduced. Now the tone becomes darker, and the leaps of thought more violent. The chimes playing their hymn-tune lead the poet to think about hymns in general—'they sing of peace, and preach despair'. In other words, what the words say is at variance with the effect they produce on us when we listen to them sung. Yet once, we are told, hymns had a function for Lowell—they enabled him to deal with the remorse he has already hinted at, and seemed to offer a chance of escape towards some kind of *au delà* which is not defined.

The alternatives to going to church are the normal occupations of an agnostic, middle-class Sunday. Stanza 8 starts by telling us this; but then, between the fourth and the fifth line, Lowell forces on the reader a wide leap in thought. The 'old lumber banished from the Temple' is the poet himself, who is 'damned' because, in the words of St Paul's First Epistle to the Corinthians, he has not charity, and is become 'as sounding brass, or a tinkling cymbal'. The 'ten candle-ends' hint, in addition, that he is a burnt-out case. At this point it is worth noting that Lowell was a convert to

Catholicism, and now seems to have withdrawn from the faith. *Waking Early Sunday Morning* tells us quite explicitly about its author's religious dilemma in the stanza which immediately follows the one which I am now discussing. The implication line 64 ('word-less sign') is that loss of faith in some way strikes at Lowell's vocation to be a poet. The leap to stanza 9 is emotionally very direct, even if syntactically somewhat oblique. God is hiding his presence little by little. His 'emblems' are trivialised, and become 'like old white china doorknobs'—outmoded things one might find in a local junk-shop. The stanza ends with a poignant allusion to Lowell's recurrent attacks of mental illness. These have formed the subject matter of some of the other poems he has written in the past ten years.

Another leap follows—from the reader's point of view perhaps the most strenuous in the poem. The tenth stanza (lines 73–80) is the one which, from Lowell's point of view, helps to set his poem in a contemporary American context, and more especially in a political context. It is at this stage that one sees most clearly the reasons for Lowell's attraction to Marvell's *Upon Appleton House*, a poem in which political discussion mingles with lyricism. Marvell is able to embrace the two extremes, and make them illuminate one another:

> For to this naked equal flat
> Which Levellers take Pattern at,
> The Villagers in common chase
> Their Cattle, which it closer rase . . .

What view does Lowell take of the American situation? *Waking Early Sunday Morning* is the first poem in a volume called *Near the Ocean*. More than half the rest of the book consists of translations, mostly from the Latin. In a prefatory note, Lowell tells the reader that 'the theme which connects my translations is Rome, the greatness and horror of her Empire'. For 'Rome', we must some-times read 'America'.

Among the Latin poems which Lowell chooses to translate are Horace's ode addressed to a friend who served with him under Brutus:

> *With you too at Philippi, at that hysterical*
> *mangling of our legions, when we broke*
> *like women. Like an Egyptian*
> *I threw away my little shield.*

Another translation is a version of Juvenal's *Satire X*, *The Vanity of Human Wishes*:

> *War souvenirs and trophies nailed to trees,*
> *a cheek strap dangling from a clobbered helmet,*
> *a breastplate, or a trireme's figurehead,*
> *or captives weeping on the victor's arch:*
> *these are considered more than human prizes.*

These translations provide a context for the second half of *Waking Early Sunday Morning*.

Lines 73–80 mingle three different sets of allusions, to David's victory over Goliath, as recounted in the *First Book of Samuel*, and to the occasion when David killed two hundred Philistines and cut off their foreskins, in order to win King Saul's daughter as his wife; to Imperial Rome; and to the military might of present day America, which Lowell thinks will go the same way as that of the Philistines and the Romans. He proves himself ingenious at finding phrases which refer forward and back to two, or even all three, of these points of comparison:

> *elephant and phalanx moving*
> *with the times and still improving.*

But the allusions do not always work satisfactorily. Take the lines:

> *little redemption in the mass*
> *liquidations of their brass.*

The primary meaning seems to be that the mass killings ordered by the brass-hats ('brass' used abruptly and colloquially, just as the Yiddish word 'dreck'* is used in line 59, will lead to no positive

* In New York slang the word is currently used in the sense of rubbish. In more traditional Yiddish the meaning is made stronger, with excremental connotations.

result. But the two lines can also, and almost as logically, be read as a description of the noise made by an army on the march. In the *First Book of Samuel*, Goliath is described as having 'greaves of brass upon his legs, and a targe of brass between his shoulders'. In fact, the lines act as a further elaboration and re-presentation of 'hammering military splendour'. And the rhythm reinforces this interpretation. The first line of the stanza consists of only the three words I've just quoted, with a repeated 'r' like the drum-roll of a military band. This 'r' is carried forward into the next three lines: 'armor . . . redemption . . . brass', and is interwoven with a succession of 'l' and 'm' sounds which suggest the wind-instruments. The rhythm gradually lightens and frees itself throughout these four linked lines, just as a march-tune would. But the sound effects are too elaborate; we tend to lose sight of the primary meaning altogether.

If this is very dense, what follows seems deliberately thin. 'Sing softer!' Lowell cautions himself, and then treats us to a string of abstractions, which he jingles together as if to emphasise their triviality: 'tenderness . . . restlessness . . . excess . . . success . . . self-deception . . . reckless caution'. Some of the phrases only hint at meaning—the 'sanity of self-deception' is a case in point. Lowell perhaps means that, with America going the way it is, the only way in which he and others who think like him can remain sane is by deliberately blinding themselves to the facts.

Stanza 11 (lines 81–8) concludes by repeating the cry 'anywhere, but somewhere else!', this time giving it an overtone of unspecified but powerful yearning. The poem then immediately returns to the phrase with which it began: 'O to break loose.' The musical. or thematic, method of construction here discloses itself very clearly. Both the major themes—that of corrupt power, and that of the longing for escape—are now to be kept simultaneously before us. Stanza 12 returns to the idea of 'grandeur', and treats it with imaginative grotesquerie.

At first Lowell is vague. 'Life's grandeur', he says, 'is something with a girl in summer'. He then moves immediately to a picture of the President of the United States (Lyndon Johnson, without question) swimming nude this Sunday morning, and shedding his cares for a moment. The vision is at once frightening, impressive and comic. And the moral is plain—grandeur is not the Presidency, nor the power that attaches to it, but the escape from responsibility. Lowell gets a curious minor effect from the concluding couplet. The violent caesura between the word 'sick' and the phrase which follows encourage us for a moment to think of the President as 'sick' in some more general way.

The last two stanzas provide a summary of what has gone before, and a kind of coda. In lines 97–104, Lowell spells out his political preoccupations. It is indeed the Vietnam War and the political state of America—the 'chance' assassination of Kennedy—that his thoughts have been moving towards as he wakes. These are the responsibilities which he, as much as the President, struggles to escape. But no escape is possible:

> *Only man thinning out of his kind*
> *sounds through the Sabbath noon, the blind*
> *swipe of the pruner and his knife*
> *busy about the tree of life . . .*

The final stanza is therefore a lament for the planet itself, and more particularly for the young Americans dying or already condemned to die in a series of police-actions all over the world—Korea, the Dominican Republic, Vietnam. The general sense is clear, but it is nevertheless hard to provide a convincing explanation of some of the details. In what sense, for example, is the planet a 'cone'? Lowell is too sophisticated a verse-technician to allow a trope of this kind to be dictated entirely by the rhyme, though one might guess that the need to rhyme probably suggested it. Yet, while we know that the earth is volcanic, and while we also know that volcanoes have a characteristic conical form, it is hard to picture a cone-shaped planet. There is, however, another possible meaning for the word 'cone', though the *Oxford English Dictionary* describes it as both doubtful and obsolete. Cone can mean 'cocoon'—in *Red Cotton Nightcap Country* Browning speaks of the 'cradle-cone' of a butterfly. One might put this together with the other possible meanings of the word—one of which might be stretched to include the idea of 'a point in space'—to achieve a reasonably plausible explanation. But it seems a long way round. There is also a minor difficulty over the exact status of the phrase 'until the end of time/to police the earth'. This must logically be applied to 'our children'. The rhythm and to some extent the grammar unhelpfully suggest otherwise.

The real crux however is reached with the last two words of the poem—'monotonous sublime'. The trouble has been prepared for by Lowell's lax use of the word 'ghost' a little earlier. The word seems more of a gesture than a description, but what Lowell seems to be suggesting is that the universe has become in some way impalpable, robbed of reality by wrong aspirations. This does not fit very happily with the vivid image of one stanza back, where earth was described as licking its sores. But it does signal, as I have said, the fact that Lowell is about to introduce us to the idea of sublimity. This notion belongs more to the poetry of the eighteenth and nineteenth century than to that of the twentieth. Pope has a definition in *The Art of Sinking in Poetry* which is cruelly apposite. 'The Sublime of Nature,' he says, 'is the Sky, the Sun, Moon, Stars, etc.' Keats speaks in a letter of 'the Wordsworthian or egotistical sublime'. The nineteenth-century moralist Samuel Smiles tells us that 'the patriot who fights an always-losing battle—the martyr who goes to his death amidst the triumphant shouts of his enemies . . . are examples of the moral sublime'. Obviously Lowell's 'monotonous sublime' must find a place among these. Equally obviously, it will not do so, because the phrase is virtually meaningless, however we try to define it, in terms of what has gone before. Of sublimity, or anything like it, *Waking Early Sunday Morning* offers two versions. It can be 'all life's grandeur', which is 'something with a girl in summer'. Or it might, more plausibly, be 'hammering military splendor', which at least embraces the notion of monotony. But neither really fits. What Lowell seems to want to say is that in embracing ideas of greatness, and especially of political and material greatness, men have tended to lose their own souls. But he does not succeed in saying it very precisely or convincingly, despite the melancholy beauty of the concluding cadences.

I have chosen to discuss *Waking Early Sunday Morning* because a flawed poem (provided always that its author is a man of talent) can often tell us more about poetry than a more perfect one. The faults speak as clearly as the virtues. *Waking Early Sunday Morning* is, quite evidently, the work of a very gifted writer, capable of an enormously subtle range of effects and equipped with a far-ranging imagination. It is also the work of a poet who is deeply and desperately concerned with the fate of the world. When he was still a practising Catholic, Lowell, as his earlier poems prove, saw the universe as something within which man was the active principle, the separable centre. Now, as a recent critic has said of his work, 'the whole universe, man, animal and thing, moves relentlessly on the same principle'.* This perhaps makes Lowell more sympathetic to most of his readers, and it gives his work a pathos which formerly it did not possess. But pathos is rather a dangerous quality in a poet—a kind of solvent in which the intellectual order dissolves.

In *Waking Early Sunday Morning*, Lowell apparently wants to substitute an external, or literary, principle of order for that internal ordering which he is no longer sure that he possesses. I have already pointed out that the poem is an attempt to adapt Marvell to the twentieth century. But this is not mere copying, it is adaptation for a purpose. Lowell's tactic, as I have said, is to wear Marvell's mask and speak through it. The diction ranges freely between Marvell's day and our own, from the contemporary colloquialism of 'dreck' to the high style of 'Sing softer!' The trouble is that modes of diction also involves modes of thought, something which emerges fairly clearly from my comments on the 'monotonous sublime'. Inconsistencies matter less than we tend to think in most poetry—the consistency of emotion or character is usually enough. But this is not true of metaphysical verse of the type which Marvell wrote, which relies heavily on the fact that all meanings are carefully limited, all verbal relationships defined. It is thus that Marvell achieves his characteristic crispness. Each paradox is also a syllogism:

> *But now the* Salmon-Fisher's *moist*
> *Their* Leathern Boats *begin to hoist;*
> *And, like* Antipodes *in Shoes*
> *Have shod their* Heads *in their* Canoes.

* Jerome Mazzuro, *The Poetic Themes of Robert Lowell*, University of Michigan Press, 1965.

Lowell is unable to limit things in this way because, like nearly all modern poets, he possesses an essentially romantic sensibility. The paradoxes blur, and the images shoot out their trendrils in all directions until this vigorous ivy pulls the stones apart, and the whole building tumbles into picturesque ruin.

The following poems are recommended for progressive study of Robert Lowell:

Early Lowell
Mother Marie Therèse (in *Poems 1938–1949*)

Lowell and madness, Lowell and responsibility
Waking in the Blue; *Skunk Hour*, both in *Life Studies*.

Further development
For the Union Dead in *For the Union Dead*.

Lowell as translator
Serving under Brutus; *The Vanity of Human Wishes* (compare with Johnson's version of the same poem), both in *Near the Ocean*.

Criticism in Action in
the Examination Room

by Dennis Welland

anyone lived in a pretty how town
(with up so floating many bells down)
spring summer autumn winter
he sang his didn't he danced his did.

5   Women and men (both little and small)
cared for anyone not at all
they sowed their isn't they reaped their same
sun moon stars rain

children guessed (but only a few
10   and down they forgot as up they grew
autumn winter spring summer)
that noone loved him more by more

when by now and tree by leaf
she laughed his joy she cried his grief
15   bird by snow and stir by still
anyone's any was all to her

someones married their everyones
laughed their cryings and did their dance
(sleep wake hope and then) they
20   said their nevers they slept their dream

stars rain sun moon
(and only the snow can begin to explain
how children are apt to forget to remember
with up so floating many bells down)

25   one day anyone died i guess
(and noone stooped to kiss his face)
busy folk buried them side by side
little by little and was by was

all by all and deep by deep
30   and more by more they dream their sleep
noone and anyone earth by april
wish by spirit and if by yes.

> Women and men (*both dong and ding*)
> summer autumn winter spring
35 reaped their sowing and went their came
> sun moon stars rain

If practical criticism has any place in the examination room it must be as an activity essentially different from the performances usually expected of candidates on these occasions. The examination system is primarily a test of knowledge acquired: in literature examinations the source of that knowledge may be all too obviously a work of criticism or the introduction to a prescribed text, well or imperfectly remembered, and reproduced slavishly, fluently or (too seldom) thoughtfully. Sometimes the answer will seem to depend only on the remembered outline of school notes, the memorised specimen answer to a roughly similar question, or the desperate attempt at wrenching totally different knowledge into some semblance of an answer to a question that has clearly come as a cruel shock to the victim. To some extent the ability to marshal information is also being tested, but this and real originality of mind will be shown, in the time allowed, only by the very best with any distinction: the examination shows primarily that the candidate has some intellectual baggage to declare, and even in English this is not negligible evidence.

'Even in English', because the study of literature ought to result in something more than the accumulation of facts. Taste and judgment are involved, but they can rarely be taught and ought not to be expected at too high a level. 'Literature as experience' has become a catch-phrase, but phrases often catch because there is some truth in them. Unlike Eliot's characters who 'have had the experience but missed the meaning', too many candidates know all too well the meaning of the books they have read, but they have missed the experience: they write about the books as they have been told, or as they think they are expected, to write, not as though the books have any reality for them.

The reader who has progressed thus far in this book needs presumably no rearguard defence of the place of literature in the syllabus, but he may greet with some surprise the suggestion that a practical criticism examination differs from others in its attempt to elicit enjoyment. Yet this is really what is wanted: not, of course, wide-eyed gushing enthusiasm of the 'magical beauty evoked by these light vowels, sombre consonants and exotic images' variety, but the intellectual satisfaction of confronting a challenge and working out unaided one possible solution to a problem. What the examiner hopes for is an interested response to an unprepared text; he does not expect an exhaustive critical exegesis of the poem, nor does he want a parlour-game of 'spot the author'. The candidate who does identify the author needs to be exceptionally careful to confine his answer to the poem given and not to augment it with extraneous information that is often not relevant to that particular piece: it is to save candidates from this pitfall, rather than out of exhibitionism or malice, that the examiner will try to choose a poem that candidates are not likely to have encountered already, but it is seldom possible to do this with absolute success. The discussion that follows is concerned with one poem that will, for many young students, meet this requirement. It is not being offered as a 'model answer' for there is no such thing at this level and in this context. Practical criticism tests individual, spontaneous reaction, and as this will necessarily differ from candidate to candidate so will the form in which each expresses his reaction and the aspects that he chooses to emphasise. I am trying to suggest only one way of coming to grips with a poem that may at first sight look intimidating but can in fact be very rewarding. To allay misgivings it had better be said at once that when on one occasion it was set as an examination piece the eccentricities of the poem gave candidates more to get their teeth into than a more conventional poem would have done. They found plenty to say about it and were often unusually percep- tive in their insights and confident in their judgments, even though (or because?) it was completely unfamiliar to them. It falls into no recognisable category and lends itself to no facile and meaningless platitudes; it requires careful reading, it necessitates thought, and it demands a response. This challenge most candidates met with a courage and a success that in part dictated its choice for discussion here, but this essay is in no sense a report on that examination nor is it based on any detailed memory or rereading of individual scripts: this passing reference to the occasion is made only to anticipate the objection that to set such a poem would be to expect too much of the candidates. In the event, we expected too little and were delighted to be put right.

The most striking feature of the poem is obviously its idiosyncrasy: the reader will quickly become aware of the contrast between the apparent regularity of the quatrain form and the irregularity of punctuation and use of capitals. This provides an immediate clue to the poem's structure, for the only two full-stops (at the end of the first and penultimate stanzas) divide it clearly into three sections. There is a one-stanza introductory statement, an unbroken narrative flow extending through eight stanzas, and a one-stanza *envoi*. That the only use of a capital letter occurs at the beginning of the same word with which the second and third sections open calls attention to a similarity which extends to the whole of those two lines, and indeed the whole of the two stanzas. The identical fourth line in both (it is echoed in a mutated form at line 21) and the absence of any punctuation mark at the end of the poem suggest that the final stanza really marks the beginning over again of the whole cycle. This of course is reinforced by the variation, in line 34, of the list of seasons that has occurred twice before; this time it ends with spring, which was where the movement began in the opening stanza (line 3). By means such as these the poem establishes the pattern of cyclical progression which is a reflection of its main theme, and by now we are in a position to define that theme as a preoccupation with the natural rhythms of life, human, seasonal and universal.

The idea of rhythm thus introduced illuminates both the marked rhythmical movement of the verse, the references to music, singing and dance, and the parenthesis in line 19. Associations with the rhythms of nursery rhymes may be helpful here, for, like the nursery rhyme's, one function of this poem is to restate in novel terms the familiar aspects of daily life so that these become at one and the same time more magical and yet more manageable. There is a similarly lyrical interplay between sense and nonsense until the apparent nonsense acquires a new sense of its own in the context of the poem's world. The process may be dignified (though not in any way distorted) by being related to 'that synthetic and magical power' which Coleridge sees as 'blending' and 'fusing' opposing concepts into imaginative unity, 'dissolving, diffusing and dissipating' in order to re-create. The poet is not merely removing 'the film of familiarity' in Coleridge's phrase, but is actively creating a new world, akin to but more sharply perceived than, the world of everyday experience. In this way it may be constructive to speak of this as a poem in the Romantic tradition, because to do so is not merely to decorate it with an academic label, but to make a positive statement about the way in which the poem works. In calling it 'Romantic' we have not said the last word on it, but we may have usefully said one of the first, provided we can show how the removal of the film of familiarity is accomplished and what is achieved in the process.

One way in which this is attempted is by putting into the reader's mind everyday phrases which, however, are not used here in their usual form. Sometimes the usual order is inverted: 'men and women' becomes 'Women and men' (lines 5 and 33), and is paralleled by 'dong and ding' (line 33). Sometimes one component is changed: 'more and more' becomes 'more by more' (line 12), 'great and small' becomes 'little and small' (line 5), and 'they dreamed their dream' becomes 'they slept their dream' (line 20) which in turn is inverted in line 30. Merely to remark this, however, is no more adequate than merely to say 'In this poem the poet plays with words' unless we are prepared to go on and to recognise that it is purposeful play that achieves a definable effect. It is not enough merely to note that parts of speech are used in non-grammatical roles, nor are such phrases as 'He does it to make us think' any help unless we can indicate the results of our thought. At this stage of the discussion it may be possible only to say that we are reminded of everyday phrases but puzzled to find them occurring in unfamiliar forms: our expectations are cheated, or left unfulfilled in rather the same way that the stanzaic form fails to live up to the regularity that it appears to promise. What looks like an orthodox rhyming quatrain employs pure rhyme only in the first couplet (and not always there, for in stanzas 5, 6 and 7 the opening couplets are assonantal approximations only). The second couplet of the stanza never gets nearer to rhyme than, for example, same/rain, summer/more, and usually makes no attempt at it. What looks familiar, ordered, tidy, turns out to be disconcerting, inconclusive: the metrical regularity so noticeable in the first two lines of the poem as to acquire a sing-song rhythm dissolves into the irregularity of the next two unrhymed lines where syntactical eccentricities of usage increase the confusion.

The idea of 'confusion' has not hitherto been introduced into the discussion because to begin with it might have given it undue prominence and might have obscured the design of the poem. The tension between confusion and order is integral to the poem's development and is in fact carefully controlled by the poet. Awareness of the confusion will probably occur much earlier in our experience of the poem, but not an awareness of the role of the confusion, and it is for this reason that detailed discussion of it has been deferred until its purpose is becoming discernible. Contrary to a popular superstition, good poetry does not set out to obscure the simple truths of life, and its resistance to comprehension is not an index to its greatness. For our purposes one of the advantages of this poem is the way in which it highlights this issue, forcing the reader (unless he is prepared to dismiss the poem out of hand) to consider how an extremely idiosyncratic—even perverse—use of language affects its power of communication. Continuing to focus on the opening stanza, for example, we can recognise the first line as a variant on the fairy-tale type of statement 'Jack lived in a pretty little cottage . . .' The folk-hero has now, however, become the undistinguishable 'anyone' whose ordinariness is emphasised by the lower-case initial letter and whose dwelling is now characteristically urban instead of rural. It is not even localised: it is a town, and a 'pretty how' town at that. 'Pretty', that is, is being given its modern colloquial connotation of disparagement, and although the statement would not readily lend itself to the old-fashioned exercise of sentence analysis, it carries far more weight than would the metrically equivalent alternative 'anyone lived in an average town' because the idea of 'prettiness' cannot be wholly excluded. The parenthesis which follows relieves the sense of ordinariness by a lyrical grace-note—even 'pretty how' towns are not wholly devoid of beauty—but the heavy 'down' on which the line ends seems to bring it down to earth again, and sets in motion that rhythm of vertical movement which, in lines 10 and 24, counterpoints the predominantly cyclic movement already noted.

This up/down antithesis also prepares us for the idea of compensatory balance that becomes increasingly important: 'what goes up must come down' but 'what you lose on the swings you gain on the roundabouts' and 'as ye sow, so shall ye also reap'. Aphorisms of this nature seem to me very close to the surface in this poem but, like the clichés, they are suggested rather than stated. What I mean by 'compensatory balance' is first exemplified in line 4. The first half of it suggests elliptically that he sang about his aspirations, the things that he did not do, but he did achieve something and got a parallel enjoyment from that ('he danced his did'). This is contrasted sharply in the next stanza with the more limited and pedestrian achievements of more ordinary people, those whose negativeness ('they sowed their isn't') merely produces more negativeness ('they reaped their same'). In this context the force of the parenthetic 'both little and small' becomes more apparent: the poet suggests the familiar antithesis 'great and small' but by substitution of 'little' implies that there are no 'great' left in the world of humdrum ordinariness.

Yet another contrast is developed in the following stanza by the suggestion that this humdrum quality is the concomitant of adult life in which children lose their pristine enthusiasm. 'Down they forgot as up they grew,' as well as lines 22–4, might be thought of as the poet's epitome of Wordsworth's *Immortality Ode*, though without, of course, the religious, philosophical and quasi-mystical undertones that enrich that poem. Even the happily married couple, whose love for each other the poem goes on to celebrate, are not unaffected by this process for they too (line 20) 'said their nevers' and 'slept their dream'. Yet—compensatory balance again—their love gave them strength to face adversities: they 'laughed their cryings and did their dance' (line 18) and ultimately (line 30) they came to 'dream their sleep' in a spirit of reconciliation reminiscent of Prospero's lines in *The Tempest*:

> *We are such stuff*
> *as dreams are made on; and our little life*
> *Is rounded with a sleep.*

It *is* a little life, the poet insists, and an imperfect one, but it need not be wholly trivial or meaningless.

The central section of the poem twice has recourse to a string of parallel phrases of what we may perhaps call an '*x* by *x*' construction. The first begins in line 12 with the 'more by more' already discussed and develops through lines 13 and 15 where the pairings reiterate the poem's concern with time, the seasons and the world of nature by referring to specific examples of these. This group culminates in 'stir by still', an economical epitome of the contrasting bustle and tranquillity, flux and stability, that dominate the poem. The second group of such phrases begins with the stillness and progresses through temporal and seasonal associations to a reassertion of the importance of love—that is, it reverses the movement of the first group. From the death of the couple and their unceremonious burial 'side by side' (line 27) the pairings become increasingly unfamiliar but increasingly positive. In lines 28 and 29 these two little people, both belonging to the past now, are irrevocably and totally buried deep down in the earth, but from this point the movement is upward through the next three lines: 'more by more' (the phrase echoes the reference to their love in line 12) 'they dream their sleep' (the importance of this inversion of the phrase in line 20 and the significance of the tense-change begin to emerge). The earth in which they are buried revives in April, just as their wish for love survives in the spirit, and the uncertainty (the 'if') of earthly life gives way to the affirmation of eternity (the 'yes'). Against this rising affirmative movement, however, is set the cyclic, equivocal rhythm of ordinary human and seasonal life which, we have seen, is inconclusively restarted in the final stanza.

By now these two movements may seem to give to the poem an ambivalence that for some readers will seem an extension of the confusion but which others will accept as a valid statement of the duality of human existence. On the one hand there is the uncaring indifference of the busy but unfulfilled 'women and men'; on the other, there is the more romantic assertion of the primacy of love for at least some of the people some of the time. Three points need to be made about the poet's attempt to reconcile these apparently contradictory views. First, the assertions about love, though rising to that emphatic 'yes' of line 32 are always qualified, never lose sight of the 'if' of the same phrase. Second, if the concept is paradoxical the deliberately paradoxical form of its expression throughout the poem conditions us at least to entertain it. Third, the pair of lovers the poet is commemorating are not Romeo and Juliet or any identified couple: they are 'anyone' and 'noone' except when, in line 17, marriage makes them 'someones' and 'everyones'—that is to say, the poet is making them not merely anonymous but, more significantly, typical; at once individual and yet generic. Read in one way, 'noone' is 'woman', 'anyone' is 'man', yet the primary meaning of both words is also exploited all the time so that a line like 'and noone stooped to kiss his face' carries two simultaneous and contrary meanings, one of human affection, the other of human isolation. It is an unusually sharp illustration of the power of poetry to say two things at once, to make us hold in our minds at one and the same time two conflicting ideas.

We can now, perhaps, summarise all this by saying that the poet is aware of and troubled by the anonymity of the individual life in modern urban society, and at the same time confident of the abiding intensity and the unique importance, to the individual, of the ordinary human emotions which are as natural, as recurrent, and as much taken for granted as the cyclic movement of the seasons and the climate. He sees ordinary everyday life as both usual and unusual, exciting and pathetic at once, and adopts towards it an attitude of childlike simplicity and wonder, paralleled by the idealisation of childhood in the poem and by the tone of nursery-rhyme whimsy which frequently modulates into a memorably simple yet moving statement of basic human feeling (as in line 16: 'anyone's any was all to her').

I have tried to make this statement—and indeed the whole analysis—as neutral as possible, though my enjoyment of the poem will probably have been apparent. Whether the candidate likes or dislikes the poem is of less consequence to the examiner than his ability to substantiate his attitude by close reference to the text and by intelligent interpretation of it. The present poem, for example, depends so much on its emotive effect that response to it is likely to be sharply divided. What I have called its affirmation of the primacy of love will seem to some readers convincing and to others senti-mental, just as to some the idiom will seem original, economical and exciting where to others it will be tricksy and meretricious affectation. A case can be made for either viewpoint or, of course, for a more moderate one in between those two extremes. The view which is cogently presented will not be penalised for not coinciding with that of the examiner, who will prefer an expression of reasoned opinion to an answer which remains demurely on the critical fence; usually, however, it is advisable to do as I have tried to, and to marshal the evidence by analysing the poem first, rather than starting from a preconceived position of either enthusiasm or distaste. To have shewn how the poem makes its effect is to command greater respect for the personal evaluation of that effect. With this poem it should be possible to reach agreement on the fusion between form and content, tone and effect, language and mood, even though we may differ in our assessment of it. For me, the way in which the idea is expressed does not make the idea more valid or more true, but it does put it in a fresh perspective that is welcome and stimulating. Something that matters to the poet has been made to matter to me.

As I said earlier, this is not put forward as a specimen of what is expected of the candidate in the artificial conditions of the examination room. No one would expect him to treat the poem so exhaustively or to marshal his argument as carefully as I have tried to marshal mine. I am, after all, discussing a poem with which I have been familiar for some years and not trying to beat the clock while committing my thoughts about it to paper. Yet, if due allowance is made for factors such as these, the exercise is perhaps not wholly irrelevant to the examination candidate whose aims and methods should be, in some respects, the same as mine.

I have tried to clarify the total meaning of the poem as a whole, though without paraphrasing it and without losing sight of the components that make up the whole. I have not needed to go outside the text of the poem; such analogies as I have drawn with other works, pertinent as I hope they are, have not been essential to the argument but merely a means of throwing extra light on it—a pedagogic habit, if you like. It has not been necessary to identify the author nor would the discussion have been radically altered by taking into account any of his other poems. They are as extraneous to the practical criticism of this poem as is the fact that he is an American (e. e. cummings) or as are the details of his biography. No attempt has been made to speculate about his intentions in writing the poem: the printed words on the page were the data and the object of this essay was a reasoned statement of the effect of the poem as a whole on one reader. The purpose of practical criticism is not to take a poem to pieces ('We murder to dissect' said Wordsworth in a different context) but to insist on its unity, to increase the reader's understanding and enjoyment of it by clarifying, not destroying, its mystery. For this reason I have not taken it aspect by aspect ('form', 'metre', 'diction', 'imagery', 'theme' etc.) but have tried to show how all these elements interact and contribute to the total effect of the poem, how our understanding of its theme depends on our response to its idiom, its tone, its structure, its form, in kaleidoscopically shifting patterns: they are all there in view all the time but sometimes one occupies our attention more than the others though always in relation to them. To set down the scansion of specimen stanzas, to say that the rhyme scheme is *a a b c*, to define the metre and point to its irregularities— these things seem to me valueless unless they can in some way be made to throw light on the poem as a whole by being related to its other facets. Form is more organic than this sort of pedantry implies, just as meaning is more complex than paraphrase can suggest.

In short, what the examiner looks for in a practical criticism exercise is not a single standard answer. He is not asking for the candidate to grade the poem according to some hypothetical Baedeker scale of excellence: the 'great' or the 'first-rate' poem will seldom be set for practical criticism, partly because the candidate may well have encountered it already, but primarily because a poem of this calibre does not lend itself so readily to analysis and discussion as does one slightly less good which allows more scope for individual response and judgment. The candidate ought not, of course, to be expected to waste his energy on a worthless or really inferior piece. This poem seems to me good enough to merit serious attention but neither so good nor so bad as to make critical discussion of it a work of supererogation: its subject and its method ought to engage the candidate's interest, and his response to it, hostile or favourable, should be capable of being expressed without self-consciousness.

In any such exercise, though the candidate is unlikely to say all that could be said about the poem, he should keep in perspective the total effect of it as a whole. This should be reinforced by an awareness of the contribution to that total effect by at least some of the features of the poem that have attracted the candidate's attention, or that seem to him to conflict with or detract from that effect. The wood should be kept in view as well as the trees, and the more that can be said about any overall design that can be descried in the wood the better.

Beyond this there are no rules for practical criticism in the examination room, and no preparation for it other than practice coupled with the sharpening of critical perception that comes with the constant widening of reading and experience.

Epilogue

The critical tips and demonstrations of critical method in the foregoing pages should assist you in giving more structure to your own responses not only to the poems included within them. For some people it may most usefully suggest a return to the practice of always reading poetry aloud, as Dr Craig proposes on p. 40. In the Middle Ages, we know, so necessary was it to pronounce what one read that monastic cells, being reading rooms, were held to be units of noise and kept away from corridors of silence.

Going further—and in no sense to undercut the work of all the contributing critics—you should ask yourself whether you have not lent an ear too readily and given your consent without thinking the problems out afresh. Critical performances are intended only as one side of a dialogue and scrupulous criticisms do not necessarily mean agreements and acceptances all the time. With such an acceptance the most radical ideas would at once become an orthodoxy and there would be not a dozen or so major poets in English but a hundred or two. A convincing personal response to literature must always possess within itself something of a heresy that likes to stand up and state the reasons for its nonconformity. This is, if you like, your task considering the sections of the present book.

Difficult as the critic's task may be, it is nothing in comparison with that of the poet who articulates in a lifetime perhaps only a small body of real poems that survive critical reading. Criticism in action only offers a powerful opinion and returns the reader to his texts with the challenge to accept if he will, but not the license to hover, temporise and be always neutral.

M.P.H.

FURTHER READING

The Poets

The following is a list of the works by poets represented in the
book. It does not include volumes available primarily in other
countries, those superseded by later collections or issued in small
numbers and probably no longer obtainable.

E. E. CUMMINGS
Complete Poems, Faber 1968
73 Poems, Faber 1964
Selected Poems 1923–58, Faber 1960
Selected Poems, Penguin 1963

DONALD DAVIE
A Winter Talent, Routledge 1957
A Sequence for Francis Parkman, Listen Records, and Marvell Press
1961
Events and Wisdoms, Routledge 1964

ROBERT GRAVES
Collected Poems, Cassell 1959
Poems 1965–1968, Cassell 1968
Poems, Penguin
See also: DOUGLAS DAY, *Swifter than Reason*, North Carolina
University Press: O.U.P. 1963

THOMAS HARDY
Collected Poems, 4th edn, Macmillan 1930
Love Poems, ed C. J. Weber, Macmillan 1963
Selected Short Poems, Macmillan 1966

TED HUGHES
Hawk in the Rain, Faber 1957
Lupercal, Faber 1960
Wodwo, Faber 1967
Selected Poems, Faber 1962

PHILIP LARKIN
North Ship, 1945; n. e. Faber 1966
The Less Deceived, Marvell Press 1955
The Whitsun Weddings, Faber 1964

D. H. LAWRENCE
Collected Poems, Heinemann 2 vols. 1964
Selected Poems, ed J. Reeves, Heinemann 1951
Poems, Penguin

ROBERT LOWELL
Poems 1938–1949, Faber 1950
Life Studies, Faber 1959
Initiations, Faber 1962
For the Union Dead, Faber 1965
The Old Glory, Faber 1966
Near the Ocean, Faber 1967
Selected Poems, Faber 1965
See also: JEROME MAZZARO, *Poetic Themes of Robert Lowell*,
University of Michigan Press: Cresset Press 1966; and H. B. Staples,
Robert Lowell, Faber 1962.

HUGH MACDIARMID
Collected Poems, Collier-Macmillan 1967
A Lap of Honour, MacGibbon & Kee 1967
See also: KENNETH BUTHLAY, *Hugh Macdiarmid*, Oliver & Boyd
1964

FRANK PRINCE
Doors of Stone, Hart-Davis 1963

ISAAC ROSENBERG
Collected Poems, Hogarth Press 1952

JON SILKIN
The Re-ordering of the Stones, Chatto, Phoenix Living Poets 1961
Nature with Man, Chatto, Phoenix Living Poets 1965
New and Selected Poems, Chatto 1966

EDWARD THOMAS
Collected Poems, 2nd ed, Faber 1949
Selected Poems, Faber 1964
See also: H. COOMBES, *Edward Thomas*, Chatto 1956

RICHARD WILBUR
Poems 1943–1956, Faber 1957
Advice to a Prophet, Faber 1962

The Critics

The following is a list of works of general literary criticism from which critical ideas may be developed.

D. S. NEWTON and R. S. RUSHTON
A Glossary of Literary Terms, rev. Abrams, Rinehart English Pamphlets, Holt, Rinehart & Winston 1957

CLEANTH BROOKS
Modern Poetry and the Tradition, Oxford U. P. 1966
The Well-Wrought Urn, Dobson 1949

CLEANTH BROOKS and ROBERT PENN WARREN
Understanding Poetry, 3rd edn, Holt Rinehart & Winston 1960

WILLIAM EMPSON
Seven Types of Ambiguity (1930), n. e. Chatto 1949; Peregrine Books

R. P. HEWETT
Reading and Response, Harrap 1960

F. R. LEAVIS
Revaluation, Chatto 1936; n. e. Peregrine Books
New Bearings in English Poetry (1932), n. e. Chatto 1950; Peregrine Books

F. R. LEAVIS, ed.
Scrutiny, 20 vols, 1932–1953. 2 vol. selection, Cambridge U. P. 1963. (Note especially essays on criticism in Vol. 1.)

C. DAY LEWIS
The Poetic Image, Cape 1957

ALEX PREMINGER, ed.
Encyclopaedia of Poetry and Poetics, Princeton U. P. 1965

I. A. RICHARDS
Practical Criticism, Routledge 1929
The Principles of Literary Criticism, 2nd edn, Routledge 1926

DENYS THOMPSON
Reading and Discrimination, Chatto 1934

JOHN WAIN, ed.
Interpretations, Routledge 1955

RAYMOND WILLIAMS
Reading and Criticism, Muller 1950

YVOR WINTERS
The Function of Criticism, Routledge 1962

For studies of the development of modern English verse see:

FREDERICK GRUBB
A Vision of Reality, Chatto 1965

ANTHONY THWAITE
Contemporary English Poetry, Heinemann 1959

THE CONTRIBUTORS

T. R. BARNES

Senior English Master, Bishop Wordsworth's Grammar School, Salisbury, author of *English Verse: Voice and Movement from Wyatt to Yeats*, Cambridge U. P. 1967; and *Poetry Appreciation*, Faber 1969

ANTHONY BEAL

Deputy Managing Director, Heinemann Educational Books, editor of Lawrence's critical writings and author of a study of the same writer.

MICHAEL BLACK

Chief Editor, Cambridge University Press.

SYDNEY BOLT

Head of English Dept., Cambridgeshire College of Arts and Technology, editor of anthologies, including *The Poetry of the 1920s*, Longmans, 1967; author of *The Right Response*, Hutchinson 1966.

H. COOMBES

Worker's Educational Association organiser, Gloucestershire, author of books on *Edward Thomas*, Chatto 1956, and *T. F. Powys*, Barrie & Rockliff 1960.

DAVID CRAIG

Lecturer in English, University of Lancaster, author of *Literature and the Scottish People*, Chatto 1961.

TERRY EAGLETON

Fellow of Jesus College, Cambridge, author of *The New Left Church*, Sheed & Ward 1966, and *Shakespeare and Society*, Chatto 1967.

ALLAN GRANT

Lecturer in Humanities, Chelsea College of Science, University of London.

PHILIP HOBSBAUM

Lecturer in English, University of Glasgow, author of three books of verse and editor of *Ten Elizabethan Poets*, Longmans 1969.

JOHN LUCAS

Lecturer in English, University of Nottingham, joint author of *Romantic Mythologies*, Routledge 1966; editor of selection of *Crabbe* in Longmans' English Series, 1967.

EDWARD LUCIE-SMITH

Critic of art and literature, translator and author of three books of poetry. His work appears in Penguin Modern Poets 6. He has also written *Thinking about Art*, Calder & Boyars 1968.

ALLAN RODWAY

Reader in English, University of Nottingham. He has edited several anthologies including *Poetry of the 1930s* (Longmans) and written a volume of poetry and *The Romantic Conflict*, Chatto 1963.

KEITH SAGAR

Lecturer in English, Extra-Mural Dept. University of Manchester, author of *The Art of D. H. Lawrence*, Cambridge U. P. 1966.

DENNIS WELLAND

Professor of American Literature, University of Manchester, author of *Arthur Miller*, Oliver & Boyd 1961, and *Wilfred Owen*, Chatto 1960.